T0294123

Also available at all good book stores

9781785316470

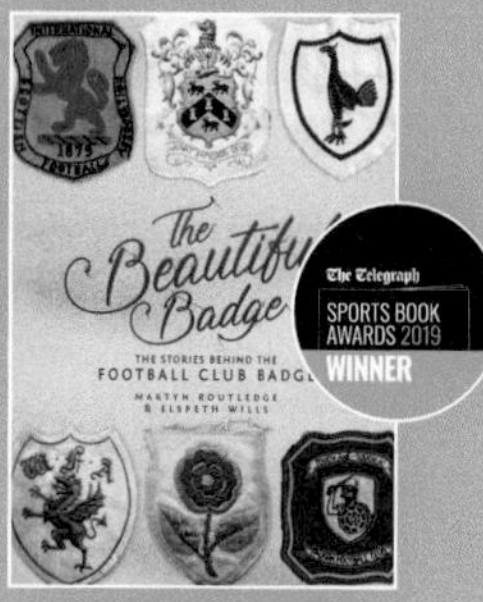

9781785313929

9781785315466

9781785317576

9781785317583

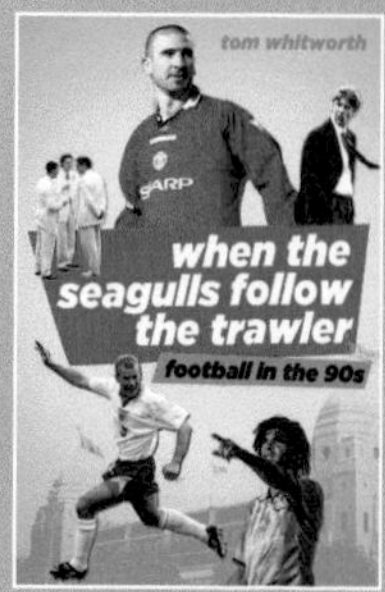

9781785317613

9781785318382

9781785318207

9781785318450

COME ON YOU BLUES

COME ON YOU BLUES

RECOLLECTIONS OF SHREWSBURY TOWN'S FIRST SEASON IN DIVISION TWO

ANDREW PRESHOUS

First published by Pitch Publishing, 2021

Pitch Publishing
A2 Yeoman Gate
Yeoman Way
Worthing
Sussex
BN13 3QZ
www.pitchpublishing.co.uk
info@pitchpublishing.co.uk

A CIP catalogue record is available for this book from the British Library.

ISBN 978 1 78531 854 2

Typesetting and origination by Pitch Publishing

Printed and bound in Great Britain by TJ Books, Padstow

Contents

Huge thanks to my dad, David Preshous, for taking me to Gay Meadow for the first time, for introducing me to Shrewsbury Town and for sharing some magnificent moments, as well as the Staines Town horrorshow. Thanks to my mum, Janet, too, for never forgetting that 'there's only one Bobby Wardle'. And of course, a massive shout-out to all the players, staff and fans of Shrewsbury Town Football Club over the years, but special praise to those who are central to this book: the boys of '79.

Foreword by Jake King

I AM very pleased to have been asked to write a few words for Andrew's book about Shrewsbury Town's first season in the Second Division, in 1979/80.

I was born in Partick and then moved to Drumchapel, Glasgow, where I played for the school and local teams. When Jock Fulton, the club's scout, told us he'd like to take a few of us for a trial at Shrewsbury, we asked him where the town was located. 'It's in England. Beside Wales,' he replied. 'Is it Welsh?' one of the lads asked. Anyway, the trial went well and manager Harry Gregg took me on as a 15-year-old apprentice in 1970. I made my debut on 10 March 1973 at Rochdale in the old Third Division. The next season, I established a regular place in the team at right-back, but unfortunately we got relegated. Town bounced straight back though and won promotion and I only missed one game. I was made captain in 1979 and went on to play over 300 league games for the club.

When I first started playing in the first team, Maurice Evans was manager, then Alan Durban came in followed by Richie Barker. When Graham Turner took over, he didn't change much, and we just kept doing pretty much the same thing. A lot of it was down to pressing. Some of the other teams would be trying to get the ball down, slow the pace and there we were – press, press, press. But we did work on our set pieces, organised our back four and pressed all the time, keeping a high tempo. And we were fit – Graham used to take us to the bottom of the Church Stretton hills and run us up to the top, all the way along and all the way down for about six and a half miles. We were fit as fleas.

We had a decent team back in the mid-to-late-1970s. Ian Atkins was a good player and Paul Maguire had the trickery on the wing, but in my opinion, the best I played with at Shrewsbury was Sammy Irvine. He once scored a hat-trick against Hereford, and John Sillett, their manager, offered £50,000 for him straight away! Overall though it was team spirit and togetherness that was our biggest strength.

Winning the championship in 1979 – what an achievement that was! Watford had some big stars such as Luther Blissett and were managed by Graham Taylor. Swansea had the Liverpool connection: Tommy Smith and Ian Callaghan, with John Toshack as manager.

When we won the title, the chairman, Tim Yates, told us that Elton John had called and wished us all the best. Little Shrewsbury winning the league – we only had about 14 or 15 players in the squad! Before the last game against Exeter, the Alltrees sport shop had offered £200 for any player who scored twice, and I got two in the first eight minutes! I put the money in the kitty and most of it went on drinks on our end of the season celebration in Magaluf. I got seven goals that season, which was pretty good for a full-back. When I scored, I used to run towards the Riverside with my right arm raised – Alan Shearer copied me!

Nobody expected us to do anything in the Second Division and even when we didn't start so well, the boss never panicked, and we didn't change our approach. We always gave 100 per cent and if you didn't, you'd be out of the team. Before that first season in the second tier, I never thought I'd play against brilliant players like Trevor Brooking and Tony Currie, England players, the type you only saw on the TV, and then there they were shaking your hand after the game. The step up also meant better hotels on longer trips, better wages, better crowds – some of the grounds we played at were brilliant, so all the matches were like FA Cup ties for us.

When you look at the clubs that were in the division at that time – Sunderland, Newcastle, Chelsea, West

Ham, all these big teams – we were beating them as well! Gay Meadow was such a tight little ground; you're right on the wall next to the Riverside so some teams were a bit intimidated when we got stuck into them. They didn't know what was happening. But sometimes I look back and think, how did we do the double over Chelsea and West Ham? We also had an excellent relationship with the fans at the time and couldn't go to the supermarket without being recognised. I remember going out one Sunday and people were coming up to me and saying, 'What a result – beating Chelsea 4-2 in front of The Shed!' It was unreal!

I'm very proud that I captained Shrewsbury when they won the championship and during the club's first season up in the Second Division. Those were fantastic times and I look forward to hearing more about it from a Town fan's perspective in *Come On You Blues*. I'm sure it'll bring back some great memories.

I expect you know that I also went on to manage Shrewsbury and later played for some of the club's biggest rivals – who really were Welsh – but that's another story!

Introduction

JUST TO be clear, I can't say I'm a diehard Shrewsbury Town supporter nowadays. I currently have a supporter number but not a season ticket. I can't even say I go to most home games in a typical season and definitely wouldn't consider going to Gillingham away on a wet Tuesday night in February. Walsall? Maybe. But I do make an effort to watch Town in the first and last game of the season, in local derbies, in matches against bigger clubs and against smaller clubs, in contests that have an impact on promotion or relegation, in cup ties, in unusual friendlies, at grounds that I haven't been to, and okay, in a sprinkling of the bread and butter fixtures that don't fit into any of the categories above, such as a mid-table clash with Gillingham at home in October (but only if it's on a Saturday). You get the picture.

From 1978 to 1980, however, it was a very different story, for that was my time as a teenage Shrewsbury Town fanboy. And as chance would have it, these were two of the most remarkable seasons in the club's history. The first was the memorable Third Division championship-winning campaign, of course. The subsequent season was Town's inaugural appearance in the second tier of English football. This was when I had a season ticket, when I went to every home game, pored over the programme and the local media reports, savoured the acts on show at Gay Meadow – famous football clubs with sizeable (and often unruly) support, football legends and younger players (and managers) going places – and marvelled at how the small squad of Town players, led by their rookie player-manager, matured and adapted to this higher level, and eventually, began to positively revel in the experience. This was when I was committed to the Salopian cause and loving (almost) every moment.

This book focuses on my recollections as a teenage football fan following Town over the 1979/80 season. This period has a significant place in the club's history, so in my view, deserves a little more coverage and attention. The account does not set out to be definitive, but rather to provide some personal impressions of that campaign. I also include some memories of supporting Salop in the years leading up to that time as well as recounting my experiences as an exiled, part-time Shrewsbury supporter in later years. Whether you were lucky enough to have been there at the time, or have just heard, read about or been bored by accounts of that halcyon period at the end of the 1970s and on into the early 80s, I hope you enjoy hearing a few more tales of the unexpected, when Town gained promotion to Football League Division Two (now the Championship) for the very first time and what happened when they got there.

1

Beginnings

Is football playing
Along the river shore,
With lads to chase the leather
Now I stand up no more?

Aye the ball is flying,
The lads play heart and soul;
The goal stands up, the keeper
Stands up to keep the goal.

A Shropshire Lad (A.E. Housman, Harrap, 1984, p42)

As Terry goes through his 1967 address book, looking up his old girlfriends:
Bob: Nancy Ridley?
Terry: Moved to Shrewsbury.
Bob: Where's Shrewsbury?
Terry: League Division Three. About six from the bottom.

(*Whatever Happened to the Likely Lads?* S1 E05: 'I'll Never Forget Whatshername', 6 February 1973)

1973/74
The Fall: Relegation

Ten months after that episode of *Whatever Happened to the Likely Lads?* aired, I went to my first Shrewsbury Town game at Gay Meadow. Terry Collier's comment was pretty close to the mark, if a little generous: Town were now second from bottom of the Third Division.

But that wasn't my first experience of a real live actual football match; that had come at Selhurst Park in September 1971. I'd gone with my friend Peter and his dad for an eighth birthday treat. Crystal Palace were totally outclassed by a Manchester United team who were on fire that day, with Bobby Charlton (later to play for Shrewsbury – really, do please read on) pulling the strings in midfield, Denis Law poaching two goals and Brian Kidd netting another. I remember George Best rounding the keeper and tapping into an empty net. I remember feeling gutted when the goal was disallowed. I still feel gutted about that moment. I have no idea who scored for Palace, and quite frankly don't really care. It was an awesome display from the Red Devils. To this day, I still can't quite believe how I didn't become an instant Manchester United fan. The highlights were on *Match of the Day* that night, but my parents said it was too late for me to stay up and watch. Fifty years on, I have just about forgiven them.

And as for Housman's evocative musings, although he wasn't referring to what was going on at Gay Meadow (the poem was published 14 years before the ground saw its first official match in 1910), for a stadium situated on the banks of the Severn, the image does fit rather nicely. But the poet wasn't a Shropshire lad, and nor am I (mind you, I am partial to the locally brewed ale named after that poem). My dad, however, can claim that accolade, having been born not half a mile from Gay Meadow and then subsequently living nearby on London Road. He occasionally mentions that his first game had been against Gainsborough Trinity in the Midland League, when he sat in the stand with his mates, excited by the small but noisy crowd and admiring the skills of players such as Jackie Butler. Other opponents that season were Frickley Colliery and Worksop Town. He also attended matches in the Third Division North and South and was privileged to witness some of the 'golden age' of Arthur Rowley, Town's prolific goalscoring legend and later manager. Dad remembers the approaches to the ground, along the English Bridge, from Coleham or Abbey Foregate, gradually filling, mostly with men in cloth caps or trilbies, walking quietly but purposefully towards the shabby, unassuming cul-de-sac ('The Narrows') that led behind the Wakeman School to the Meadow. It sounds like a scene from a Lowry painting – blimey, talk about a different era! In 1962 my dad's studies and then a career in education took him away from the area but after he got a job back in South Shropshire in 1973, he was eager to renew his acquaintance with Gay Meadow and share it with his sons.

My old man didn't exactly say "Follow the Town and don't dilly dally on the way" but he was certainly steering us in the right direction, hoping that we wouldn't fanny around too much over the important decision on who to support.

Thankfully I hadn't become a rabid Manchester United fan but I had plumped for another United – Leeds, partly as I copied my mate Ian in supporting them and mostly because they were pretty damn good. I hadn't shown much passion for following the local team, Reading, where we lived at that time, but I had enjoyed my four visits to Elm Park. I can even recall the smell of the Huntley and Palmers factory as we travelled to the ground. I did have a fondness for the blue-and-white-hooped strip but didn't really develop a strong taste for the Biscuitmen. I was happy sticking with fig rolls or Garibaldi.

So when Dad took me and my brother Steven to watch Shrewsbury v Chesterfield in early December 1973, I'd like to think I was an eager, open-minded ten-year-old hoping that Town would provide the thrilling experiences involved in supporting your local team, and that this could potentially blossom into a challenging, yet ultimately rewarding long-term relationship. Looking back, it may not have been the most auspicious time to attempt to create this bond. Up to this point the Shrews had won twice in 18 games and were second from bottom in the Third Division table. The omens weren't heeded though, and the keen young fans witnessed a continuation of the woeful form. It was a dreadful performance resulting in a 1-0 loss before a paltry crowd of 1,397.

Even at such a tender age I was learning that part of the deal when you signed up to support a lower-level team usually involved a disproportionate share of miserable moments like this. And, of course, more bleak times lay ahead so perhaps it was good to be exposed brutally to such disappointments early on in order to become acclimatised, to keep expectations in check. But maybe if I stuck with this local team-supporting project, you never know, it might just yield some exhilarating high points too. Unfortunately for manager Maurice Evans, further opportunities to experience the ebbs and flows of Shrewsbury Town Football Club were not possible – he got the chop after the game.

Despite the desperate outlook at this point in the season, there were some shoots of hope, mainly in the form of one man: Alan Durban. Acquiring this established midfielder from Derby County in September had been quite a coup for the club as the Welshman certainly had pedigree, winning a First Division championship medal under Brian Clough and representing Wales 27 times. For a young Town fan, the impact of this player's arrival was nothing short of amazing – he had appeared in sticker albums and scored goals on *Match of the Day*! While at Shrewsbury, Durban's colour photo from *Shoot!* featured prominently on the inside cover of my silver jubilee scrapbook along with a brief handwritten profile. On the opposite page there were smaller, black and white photos of other Town players obtained from the *Shropshire Star* with briefer profiles, which seemed to reflect the football fame hierarchy.

Durban took over as caretaker manager and the team's form improved but I wasn't at the next home game on Boxing Day when Town beat Watford 3-2 in front of 3,875. However, later that week we were back for Cambridge with my mum coming along too. We savoured my first win with goals from the two Alans, Tarbuck and Durban. The former was a winger who had scored a respectable number of goals for Crewe, Chester and Preston and chalked up a few more for Salop. Playing at number five against Cambridge that day was Graham Turner who, later in the decade, would contribute significantly to an upturn in the club's fortunes.

I was back for Halifax in January 1974, and a 2-0 defeat. Not much entertainment for the 2,500 or so fans at that one. Undeterred, we turned up to see Port Vale at home two weeks later. On that occasion, a grubby, adolescent Vale yob, took an immediate dislike to me and the shiny new silk Town scarf I was wearing and proceeded to pin me up against some railings just outside the ground. Luckily, my friend's dad, our local vicar, was on hand to grab the spotty lout by the scruff of his collar and told him, using distinctly non-religious terminology, to buzz off. I'd been assaulted but had escaped unscathed.

The match was terrible, and Shrewsbury were beaten 1-0. The crowd was 2,771. I was well smitten.

The less than engaging performances on the pitch and encounter with the Staffordshire oik hadn't put me off but I only returned to Gay Meadow once more that season and by then Durban had been confirmed as manager. That game against Brighton was certainly eventful: the away team's goalkeeper Peter Grummitt was carried off injured and they also had a player sent off. Town's black-bearded, piratical-looking, swashbuckling left-back, Laurie Calloway, blasted in a cracking goal, the team's first in five league games. It was a huge relief when the final whistle blew to seal the first win in 11, going back to that victory over Cambridge just after Christmas. The home supporters cheered loudly as the exhausted players (well, those who were still on the pitch) trooped off down the tunnel. Rather embarrassingly, the players then had to troop back up the tunnel and out on to the pitch again when the referee, K.W. Baker from Rugby, realised he'd blown too early. Thankfully, the score remained the same and two important points were gained. I wondered what Brighton's manager, Brian Clough, made of all the kerfuffle. A few months later, Old Big 'Ead would be back at the top end of the Football League with Leeds United, but his stay in Yorkshire would be brief.

Ultimately for Town, though, losses to Southport, Halifax and Oldham in subsequent matches left the club entrenched in the bottom four, unable to claw themselves out of the mire. Annoyingly, Port Vale finished one place above the drop-zone. My first experiences supporting Shrewsbury had ended in relegation to the Fourth Division. The last time the club had played at this level was 1959. Great timing. Would I be back for more next season? You betcha.

1974/75
The Rise: Promotion

The two attacking players who Durban had signed from Stourbridge in the close-season, Phil 'Chic' Bates (more of whom later) and Ray Haywood, didn't take long to make an impact, both netting their first goals in the second game. They went on to a grab a hatful over the season, making their mark during that successful campaign. In fact, the duo were up there with my favourite double acts of the time, better than Laurel and Hardy and Abbott and Costello (whose films were shown frequently on telly back then) and almost on a par with Ronnie Barker and Ronnie Corbett. Starsky and Hutch would soon blow all these contenders out of the water when they hit British TV screens in 1976.

I got off to a slow start in the 1974/75 season, unlike the team, who had shot to the top of the table after a seven-game unbeaten run. The Hartlepool match in early October was the first I attended, and it ended in a 1-0 defeat. Great. Most of the other home fixtures I went to that season were triumphs though – Brentford (1-0), Barnsley (3-1), Southport (1-0), Newport (1-0), the thumping of Northampton (6-0 – the biggest win I had witnessed until Gillingham came to the New Meadow in 2008 and lost by seven, equalling Town's record league victory) and Rotherham (3-1). The only other home loss I saw was the top-of-the-table clash with Mansfield (who went on to become champions) before 8,913, the highest attendance I'd been part of at Gay Meadow up to that point. Against Walsall in 1961, 18,917 had jammed into the stadium, setting a record for the ground. That was before my time, but I do have the programme, obviously.

In 1975 the team clinched promotion in second position, but the most unforgettable game that season was the bonkers 7-4 defeat of Doncaster Rovers. 'What a match' was the caption in my silver jubilee scrapbook along with Bob Davies's match report from the *Shropshire Star* on 3 February 1975, with its headline 'Haywood leads Gay Meadow goal riot'. It was only 2-0 at half-time, then Town went 4-1 up before Rovers brought it back to 5-4, but two late goals completed what was indeed, a goal riot. It was also a notable home debut for

Alex McGregor, who nabbed two. The Scottish winger's tenure at Shrewsbury may have been over in a flash but is remembered for some flamboyant flourishes.

My early years at the Meadow had been spent in the Enclosure where my dad used to take me and my brother. We'd take up positions behind the wall at the front of this section, the players' tunnel nearby and facing the Riverside terraces across the pitch, with the trees that lined the Severn poking up above the stand. Our central location offered perfect views of the playing area. At this time, away to the right behind the goal were the rowdiest home supporters – the singing, chanting, shouting contingent, the ones with thin silk scarves tied around necks or wrists: aka the Station End aggro. Here this smallish, loudish, laddish cohort would cordially invite visiting fans to come and have a go if they thought they were hard enough or suggest that the same travelling group would be going home in a flipping ambulance. Welcome to Shropshire. This rather ramshackle part of the ground was later designated as the away section.

The Enclosure was home to a character more than capable of generating his own distinctive sound and fury. A man known as 'Anti-tank' was a master at rattling off a stream of invective towards the officials, the opposition and on occasions, a hapless Town player who had just made a wayward pass. It was quite entertaining, but you did fear for your eardrums if this chap suddenly pushed forward to launch one of his verbal missiles in your vicinity.

In later years, we migrated to the Riverside, often perching ourselves on a pitchside wall near the corner adjoining the Wakeman End (referred to by some as the Tech End), but far enough away to avoid the unpleasant aroma emanating from the rather basic toilets situated nearby. I can't recall these conveniences having facilities available to dry your hands. Or to wash them, for that matter. Whatever. This was a football ground, not a hospital. More importantly, we did have a fine view of the old blue scoreboard, where a chap climbed a ladder, then manually 'loaded up' the half-time scores in the gaps A-X. From our mid-teens we ventured up to the noisier part of the Riverside terraces (which now housed the former Station End aggro), just below the buffet, where we could sing our allegiance to the team or aim disparaging chants at the away end. A home goal invariably led to a mini surge, causing a temporary displacement from your original position before order was quickly restored. In the closing stages of a game, we'd merge with the general throng of fans heading towards the Wakeman End exit, often congregating behind the goal to will the Town on for the last few minutes and joining in with the stirring renditions of 'Come on you Blues' that echoed around the ground.

As well as keeping cuttings from matches I'd attended, the programme was also an essential accoutrement to purchase, scrutinise and caress. The A5-size programme in 1973/74 set you back 5p with the cover depicting two faceless orange (it wasn't amber) and white figures tussling for a high ball. The number five was in a striped top so presumably the other player was meant to be the Town keeper. To the right of the image was the loggerheads badge and motto. This was bordered in blue and white with the club name at the top. Match details were in simple black text between the players' legs. I preferred this design to the subsequent three programme front covers. Next to the line-ups in the centre were prominent adverts for local institutions: Wem Best Bitter and Sidoli's Restaurant. The programme also contained a supplementary publication, *League Football* (formerly *Football League Review*), which I considered an inconvenience as it kept dropping out of the main feature, making me think that two publications for one game was unnecessary. However, I did appreciate the colour pics, which showcased the variety of the league. One edition that season (number 819 for the obsessives – we know you're out there) had Keith Newton of Burnley in action on the cover, City's Franny Lee inside as well as Jeff Wealands and Jimmy McGill of Hull guarding a near post. There were West Brom and Everton team groups and a view of Swindon's County Ground. On the back cover was an ad for Park Drive tipped cigarettes with a Kop-like backdrop of fans holding red and white scarves.

For the Fourth Division season of 1974/75, the front cover of the programme had Shrewsbury printed in capitals six times in blue and amber and placed diagonally with Town FC below the lowest one, just above the match details. This design wasn't going to win any awards, but its simple, visual impact does the job. For the following two years, the cover showed the three loggerheads with the latin motto, Floreat Salopia below. In 1975/76 the leopards were given a metallic bronze colouring on dark blue. The next season, the creatures gained an amber hue and the blue became lighter which brightened and improved the cover. Throughout this period, Wem Best Bitter and Sidoli's retained their advertising space in the centre pages. After this season, however, I wouldn't need to worry about the *League Football* supplement dropping out of my main programme, as its publication came to an end. It had ceased to be. I'd miss those lovely colour snaps, mind.

2

Settling in and a few flirtations

TOWN WERE back in the Third Division. I was 11 at the start of the 1975/76 season and over the next three years, my visits to Gay Meadow to support the local team became more frequent, even if my dad was unable to go, or more likely didn't really fancy spending his valuable time off work watching another soul-destroying home defeat against Chesterfield. I took up any opportunity to cadge a lift offered by the Davies family, Minor's dad, Derv's dad or even the odd school outing (the Welsh Cup semi-final replay against Wrexham in 1977; won 4-1) and was thankful to all those who ferried me to games. I was particularly grateful to get to those magical evenings under the floodlights at the Meadow, when a late return to Lydham, 20 miles away, on public transport just wasn't an option.

During this period, my life was dominated by the beautiful, and not so beautiful, game. After school, at weekends and during holidays, if I wasn't attending live football or watching football on TV, I would be playing epic four to seven-a-side games with my chums in a muddy garden behind the vicarage in Bishop's Castle and at 'the plays' (the local recreation ground) or was occupied with some other football-related activity indoors. I spent hours contentedly perusing my programmes, magazines and stickers or devising and playing out imaginary competitions using the cardboard team tabs from *Shoot!* (or homemade versions) and a pair of dice. Then there were the more competitive options – the board game Soccerama was far more relevant and engaging than Cluedo or Monopoly. A more physical activity inside the home with my brother involved booting, heading and saving a small sponge ball in a cramped hallway, but this pastime often didn't end well. On frequent occasions the action suddenly switched disciplines and descended into all-in wrestling.

But that was nothing compared to the explosive drama on the Subbuteo pitch. That is while we still had a green cloth Subbuteo pitch to compete on. When younger, I'd been very envious of school-mates who'd been given more expensive gifts such as a Tonka toy car or Scalextric. Striker seemed to be the higher-end football equivalent and seemed much more sophisticated than the alternatives – I mean, pushing the head down to kick was just so much more lifelike than flicking to kick! We ended up with Subbuteo, and not wanting to sound ungrateful, we eventually grew to love it. A bit too much at times. We started out with Hasbro's basic version with a team in red and white (Manchester United) and one in blue and white (Everton) but when we realised that other team kits and further accessories were available, soon became obsessed with adding to our collection. Many years later, Half Man Half Biscuit captured it perfectly by singing about their yearning for a Dukla Prague away kit for Christmas. For no apparent reason I coveted the West Ham away kit of claret hoops on a light blue top. My wish was granted, and we also added other heavyweight teams: Newcastle, Chelsea, Leeds, the green-topped West Germany away strip, a referee and linesmen, small trophies and better goalposts to a large box housing all the kit. We stopped short of crowd figures and a stand as that just got in the way.

Steven and I would lay down the green cloth in the front room and line up the opposing teams. We'd adapted the 'flicking' rules so you could also use finger and thumb to push the figures on bases towards the ball or around the pitch. If any purists had been looking on, they would have been irked. Games rarely lasted the full duration, as decisions were constantly challenged, goals disputed and squabbling ensued. The tiny players took the brunt of it as they were stamped on or leant on, sometimes inadvertently, but more often than not with malicious intent. Heads were snapped off or, in the ultimate misfortune, legs were severed just above the ankles. You had to feel for the tiny plastic footballers – these were more than niggles; the poor lads wouldn't be coming back from these injuries in a hurry. Meanwhile, abuse was hurled, which usually led to hand-to-hand combat. As Steven and I grappled on the living room floor, further collateral damage to the figures was inevitable as they got crushed in the fraternal fracas. After one particularly messy encounter, my dad decided to intervene and quietly, but determinedly, ripped the cloth pitch in half. Match abandoned. Subbuteo competitions were put on hold for quite a while after that. And when they did resume, the depleted teams meant five-a-side tournaments were far more common.

Back in the real world of football matches between human beings, in the three seasons (75/76–77/78) I experienced a fair share of stinkers, as noted in my 'Matches I've been to' exercise book, often standing in the cold, on terraces that were not overpopulated: Brighton, 'a dull match' lost 2-1; Walsall, 'An unmemorable match' 0-0; Lincoln, 'This was a poor match' lost 1-0. Unpleasant afternoons like those were often written into small-town, lower-league supporters' contracts with their club but there were positives too. Under Durban's stewardship, Town had developed into a decent Third Division outfit capable of defeating some of the best teams they faced at this level. In fact, this period featured several pleasurable occasions in which local rivals were beaten in front of passionate Gay Meadow crowds.

27 December 1975
Shrewsbury 2 (Durban 2) Hereford United 1
Attendance: 9,488

20 March 1976
Shrewsbury 3 (Atkins pen, Irvine, McGregor) Cardiff City 1
Attendance: 7,573

12 February 1977
Shrewsbury 3 (Kearney 2, Hornsby) Wrexham 2
Attendance: 10,487

These memorable events were no doubt formative in shaping and cementing a strong connection to Shrewsbury Town, not just for me but probably for many others too. The scorers in those games all played a part in my burgeoning fandom: Durban and McGregor have been mentioned previously; Ian Atkins had broken into the team in 1975 and would achieve legendary status at the club, to be recounted later. Sammy Irvine, the Glaswegian midfielder with the classic feather cut, took quite a lot of stick from Shrewsbury fans, often unjustified in my view, as he was clearly a very good player – I saw him score some brilliant goals including a hat-trick against Hereford (recalled by Jake King in the foreword to this book). Anyway, Irvine confounded any critics by later going on to help Stoke City gain promotion to the First Division and playing at the highest level. Sadly, his football career ended far too soon after a car crash.

Mike Kearney, with his flowing rock star locks, was also a popular figure and scored a commendable 41 goals for Town over a four-year period. Brian Hornsby had put on an actual Arsenal first team kit and made over 20 appearances, scoring six goals for the Gunners, so when he signed for Shrewsbury in May 1976 for £40,000, expectations were high. Over the next two years this skilful midfielder didn't disappoint: Hornsby, a maestro of the long-range shot or free kick outside the box, scored with 'a brilliant lob' against Wrexham. In the 6-1 rout of Portsmouth the following season (which featured an Atkins hat-trick), his magical trickery reached new levels, as recounted in my match report, 'Hornsby hit a shot into the side netting and the referee allowed it as a goal.

It was great.' Magic, our Brian. It *was* disappointing, however, when Jack Charlton lured him to Sheffield Wednesday in March 1978.

During these three seasons, there was also an appreciation of the opposition's contribution to my entertainment: Bradley of Peterborough 'scored a brilliant o.g.', 'Swindon's old-timer John Trollope scored a beauty, but it was disallowed', 'Steve Peplow of Tranmere was sent off for a handling offence' and 'Phil Holder of Palace missed a penalty'. Thanks, fellas.

Shrewsbury had consolidated their place as a solid, mid-table Third Division team, finishing ninth in 75/76, tenth in 76/77 and 11th in '77/78. It appeared to be a slight downward trajectory but during this period the team had hovered in the promotion places on a few occasions too, seeming to flirt with the concept, not quite certain if they were ready or willing to make a move. Yet by early 1978 significant changes in personnel were looming, which probably scuppered any outside chances of ending up in the top three. Not only was Hornsby, one of the star players, soon to be transferred, but other important figures were also about to move on as well.

At this time, my primary source of any news about the club was the *Shropshire Star* newspaper, which was delivered to our back door on weekday evenings. I would scour the back pages for news on the county's pre-eminent football team, while chuckling to myself if Telford had taken 'a caning' by say, Hastings (3-0; 14 January 1978). Throughout 1977/78, I snipped and pasted all the Town match reports from the *Star* into my scrapbook. Some of the headlines shocked me (but those ones may have provoked some low-level gloatage for Telford fans): 'Swindon splash out £30,000 for Bates' (Friday, 20 January 1978); noooooooo. Followed a few days later by 'Durban must buy to plug the Bates gap' (Monday, 23 January 1978); yeessssss. And soon after, splashed on the front cover of the local paper, came the *coup de grâce*, 'Durban joins Stoke City' (Monday, 13 February 1978). Crap on it. The exiting Town manager also offered coach Richie Barker the job as his assistant at the Victoria Ground, but instead he stepped up to become Shrewsbury boss, making his managerial entrance against Swindon Town. 'Barker's debut hopes end in 60 seconds of agony' (Monday, 27 February 1978). Town lost 3-2. It was also reported in the *Star* that Barker 'was encouraged by the overall performance'. Well, he would say that, wouldn't he? At least Telford got caned again that day, 4-1 away at Grantham. Perhaps I felt demoralised, but I didn't keep a *Shropshire Star* cutting when Irvine followed Durban to Stoke that July. Or perhaps I was just away on holiday.

Summer 1978, a new campaign was imminent and 'everyone knew this was the season Town would return to the lowest league level' (Jones, 1995, p.92). A sweeping statement perhaps, though key figures had left the club, so this did seem like a realistic appraisal. But it's not quite how it panned out.

1978/79
Triumph: The Spirit of 79

Shrewsbury Town's most successful season kicked off in low-key fashion. The mid-August opening fixture against Brentford drew a meagre crowd of 2,346, but it started with a win, Atkins converting a penalty for the only goal. My match report seemed rather harsh, with my expectations quite high, 'It was a bad game, not a very good start to the season.' Our team had won, kept a clean sheet – what was I expecting?!

Over the next few weeks, Town's impressive start to the season continued, so a group of my friends and I decided that it would be a bit different to cycle from Bishop's Castle to Shrewsbury to watch a game. This wasn't just for the pleasure of enjoying the rolling (and not so rolling) hills of South Shropshire on a 40-mile round trip, but also to earn some credits towards the Bronze Duke of Edinburgh Award. My small, red desk diary records the event on 4 November 1978, 'Biked to

Salop with Puck, Gerald, Snowy, Bisto and S. Walker. Went to Salop 0 Carlisle 0. Terrible match. Biked home and got really knackered near the end. Went to a bit of a firework display. Came home, really really tired and watched *Match of the Day*.' I have little memory of that day, but it's pretty safe to say that I had suffered through a gruelling ordeal. I enjoyed the bike ride though. Badum tish.

Later that month, when Richie Barker was prised away to become assistant manager to John Barnwell at Wolves, there were serious concerns that Town's form would dip. Perhaps the new caretaker player-manager bounce hadn't been factored in though because after Graham Turner took on that role, and was later confirmed as manager, Town remained undefeated until March. At the end of 1978, the Third Division table showed Shrewsbury nicely poised in second spot behind Watford. Considering the pessimistic outlook the previous summer, this was nothing short of astounding, but could it be sustained until May? January 1979 brought snowy weather and some dramatic FA Cup distractions (to be indulged in later) but Town's strong league form continued. However, after the cup exit in mid-March, there were distinct signs of wobblings with 5-0 and 3-0 defeats at Blackpool and Bury.

At kick-off time on Tuesday, 24 April, Town lay in fifth place after four consecutive draws, even though these included commendable results against Swansea and Watford, the top two teams. The home game with Tranmere now felt like crunch time and when the visitors scored first, 'it looked like the promotion dream was fading' as I recounted in my match report. Yet, the 'Spirit of 79' was kicking in, fuelled by the ardent Gay Meadow support, who having feasted on a tremendous giant-killing FA Cup run, had developed a taste for success and were now baying for league glory. After the setback of conceding the opening goal, I went on to describe the response, 'Shrewsbury played brilliantly. Trevor Birch scored with a clever lob and Paul Maguire grabbed the winner with a cracking shot much to the delight of the fans. The last 20 minutes in this game were probably as exciting as any I have ever seen at Gay Meadow.' The promotion dream was back on, and though I didn't know it at the time, in less than a month, there would be even greater Meadow memories to savour.

There was one more bump in the road though as a few days later Town lost away at promotion rivals Gillingham. The month of May would now be a five-game run-in to claim one of the three coveted spots. Victories over Lincoln and Bury and a draw at Mansfield left Town in fourth place, one point off the leadership with two home games remaining, and crucially, a game in hand over the top two, Watford and Swansea. There were 8,450 of us to cheer on our local heroes against Rotherham. Jake King scored early, but after the visitors equalised, it was tense until the last ten minutes when Tong, then Maguire added to the tally and 'by this time the crowd were very excited'. That was putting it mildly as Town were now on the verge of an historic achievement.

By the final home game, Shrewsbury lay in third place. Watford and Swansea were one point ahead but had completed all their fixtures. If Town beat Exeter then they would go up as champions; a defeat and Gillingham could still edge us out of the top three and all would be lost. This would be my 18th home league game of the season. I hadn't seen us lose at Gay Meadow since February 1978, Richie Barker's first match in charge. To say it was all set up nicely would be an understatement.

On 17 May 1979, 14,441 crammed into the ground on the banks of the Severn. There was speculation that many more were present than the official figure given. As a young fan, it was a tremendous feeling to wave the Shrewsbury Town flag (signed by David Tong, Jackie Keay and A.N. Other) with immense pride as we cheered on our heroes, invoking the 'Spirit of 79' to get us over the line. The home team couldn't have got off to a better start when the corner near-post-flick Jake King header routine opened the scoring but 'disaster struck' when the away team drew level. In my account of the game, I went on to describe how this response 'stunned the crowd but they were happy by half-time because King had scored another header and Atkins had converted a penalty'. When Tong scored the fourth near the end, the championship was in the bag. My match report contained slightly more detail than usual, 'At the end thousands of people spilled on to the pitch and celebrated for a long time after the match. It was brilliant. At last we had won promotion to the Second Division. It was the biggest crowd I had seen at the Gay Meadow.' Back of the net.

In his seminal history of Shrewsbury Town Football Club, *Breathe on 'em Salop,* Mike Jones recalled how the first congratulatory phone call to club chairman Tim Yates came from Watford chairman Elton John, even though the latter's beloved team had been well and truly pipped for the title. Yates was frank in saying, 'I don't know if I could have done that.' But that was all hypothetical. Shrewsbury Town were now champions of the Third Division.

Some of the subsequent newspaper headlines focused on the scorer of two of the goals with 'King Jake!' or 'King-size Champions', while others went for

'We are the Champions', 'Champions' or 'Champion'. Another just said 'Super Town'. My favourite is the one that has the words 'Shrewsbury in Division Two for First Time' in black text in the top-left corner, with a red banner below and 'Promotion' in white lettering. On the right is a hot air balloon in blue and amber stripes with the words 'Up Up and Away'. Taking up half the page is a colour picture of the squad superimposed on the names of teams Town will face the following season. Love it. Another popular image from the time showed boss Graham Turner chomping on a large cigar and quoted as saying, 'I'm enjoying the good times while I can, because I'm sure there will be plenty of bad times around the corner.' I cut out and kept all the reviews, photos and headlines I could get my hands on.

At this time in my life, apart from football, the only other element really competing for my attention was music (my wife Jo might contest that nothing much has changed!) I had been avidly following the charts since about 1973 and was now taping as much as I could from Radio 1 or Radio Luxembourg on Winfield, TDK or Dixons cassettes and always watched *Top of the Pops*. I liked to think my tastes had matured from the early days of 'Snoopy vs The Red Baron' by The Hotshots (my first 7in single, I'm pained to admit), Slade and Mud and were becoming more refined. When Salop won the league in May 1979, 'Pop Muzik' by M clearly deserved its high placing in the charts, but the risible efforts by Boney M, Abba and Racey, which also featured in the Top 20, were patently kids' stuff. I was quite partial to a bit of Amii Stewart, Eruption or Earth, Wind and Fire as disco never sucked for me, but it was a period when music and youth culture seemed more tribal. The only singles in the charts I had paid money for were 'Banana Splits' by The Dickies and The Undertones' 'Jimmy Jimmy' and although my tastes were much narrower back then, I was fully attuned to the chart action of the time. Further down the listings that week, a new entry at 51 and destined to go a lot higher, was McFadden & Whitehead's catchy number, 'Ain't No Stoppin' Us Now', which seemed to capture the mood created by the local football team perfectly. Town were on the move. We'd got the groove.

3

1979/80: Football League Division Two

Prelude

Shrewsbury Town had been founded in 1886 and, according to the official history of the club (Jones, 1995, p.7), played their first competitive match at Ditherington Flower Show in a six-a-side game. The club progressed from the Shropshire and District League to the Birmingham League, then on to the Midland League before gaining election to the Third Division (North) in 1950. It was now August 1979 and Town were about to launch their inaugural campaign in the second tier of the Football League.

Town fans had been spoilt rotten the previous season – clinching the Third Division championship on a heady night in May in front of over 14,000 delirious home fans was the pinnacle, but the FA Cup run had been pretty decent too. Beating Malcolm Allison's Manchester City in front of the *Match of the Day* cameras was also a standout, with David Coleman's excited commentary proclaiming that 'the stands at Gay Meadow are shaking' after Chapman glanced in Maguire's corner for the winning goal. Watching hordes of disgruntled Mancunians tramping along the railway line towards the station was a sight to behold. And any Salop fan who was at Molineux to witness Ian Atkins' ice-cool 85th-minute penalty to equalise against Wolves in the quarter-final won't forget that moment either. Even now, viewing these clips on YouTube brings a warm tingle. Cripes, Town even won the Welsh Cup too, beating Wrexham over two legs. It had been the most successful season in the club's history. So, for a teenage football nut, the anticipation levels for the new season were turned up to 11.

The 'Spirit of 79' had propelled Shrewsbury Town to the lofty heights of the Second Division so Chelsea, Newcastle and West Ham would soon be heading to Gay Meadow. I was 15 and the proud owner of a junior season ticket. It cost £12. Bring it on!

Home Matchday 1
'Reasons to be Cheerful Part 3'

Pre-season had indicated positive signs with wins against

Torquay, Exeter, Oswestry and a 4-0 thumping of First Division Wolves, with only one defeat, at Walsall. Friendlies aren't always reliable pointers though – the first competitive game at Fourth Division Halifax in the League Cup first round would hopefully provide a more accurate gauge and also a winning start to maintain the previous season's momentum.

Drawing 2-2 at The Shay didn't exactly set down a marker but did give Town every chance of progressing in the return leg, the first home game of the season. Naturally, the club were still basking in the glory of the previous campaign (well, why wouldn't you?) so Graham Turner appeared on the cover of the *Town Times* programme for the Halifax match, holding his Third Division Manager of the Year award next to the championship and Welsh Cup trophies and doing his able best not to look too smug. The first 'Pro File' article was on captain Jake King. This feature listed the subject's complete career to date, showing their appearances against different clubs season by season. Statto heaven. Atkins got the only goal of the game and the club were now primed and ready to embark on their Second Division journey.

The opening fixture pitted two 1978/79 promotion rivals together at Vetch Field. In his manager's notes, John Toshack emphasised that Swansea had not played at this level for 15 years and he also drew attention to Shrewsbury's 'first ever venture outside the lower divisions'. 'Tosh' made a point of congratulating 'Graham Turner and his team and wish them every success in Division II after today!' He got his wish as the Swans won with two late goals.

21 August 1979
Shrewsbury 1 Notts County 1
Attendance: 7,369

Okay, it wasn't the moon landings, a royal jubilee or the anniversary of the discovery of the source of the Limpopo river, but the significance of the event wasn't going to be overlooked by the philatelic industry. So sure enough, as number four in the Official Football League Series, a commemorative first day cover was issued for Shrewsbury Town's 'First Home Match Ever in Division Two' on 21 August 1979. On the envelope was the club's name and two loggerhead badges emblazoned in blue and amber next to a picture of the castle. Below was an image of a Roy of the Rovers-style footballer in Town kit athletically booting an old-style case ball. And lo and behold, there were depictions of the Third Division championship trophy and Welsh Cup again, capped off with the match result and a stamp of authenticity. The glory-basking continued.

In *Town Times* for that first home league game against Notts County, a writer for the *Sunday People* had signalled 'gloom for Shrewsbury Town supporters' by predicting that the team would end up bottom of the division. The opening-day defeat at Swansea hadn't really done anything to dispel this outlook and suggested that a long, taxing season lay ahead.

So called 'experts' aside, not everyone thought Town would go straight back down again. Oh no. Well, not in my circle of family and friends anyway. In my 'Prediction Book' dated 17 August 1979, I had listed my forecasts for the order of the First and Second Division tables, the promotion winners in the Third and Fourth Divisions, who would play in the FA Cup and League Cup finals and the Scottish League and Cup winners. It took up two whole pages of a beige-coloured exercise book. Personal football nerdism was one thing but I'd also canvassed the views of my brother Steven, friends Pogle, Boris and Nige and even my dad, who had also made their two-page contributions. I didn't ask my mum, that would have been going too far. The point is that all the predictions had Salop finishing above the three relegation spots. Two of the selections had Town in ninth and two had them sitting comfortably in mid-table. I was a little more cautious and plumped for 16th with only my dad, perhaps with a firmer grip on reality, predicting that it would be more of a struggle, with a placing in 18th (out of 22).

Incidentally, we all got it right that Sunderland would get promoted and every single one of us also predicted the First Division champions that season too. It was Liverpool, of course. Our predictions for the 1978 World Cup hadn't been quite as successful, just like Brazil, the team Steven and I thought would win. At least I had gone for Argentina losing in the final, whereas my brother may have got carried away with the brouhaha surrounding Ally MacLeod's Tartan Army and chose Scotland. Despite the fact that Andy Cameron's record became a Top 10 hit involving a lot of marching (and singing), it transpired that nobody was shaken up, they didn't win the World Cup and Scotland weren't the greatest football team.

When Town ran out for their first home Second Division match, optimism and excitement was in the air for over 7,000 fans. With Graham Turner as player-manager, the high-achieving team from the previous season was largely unchanged with the injured Paul Maguire the only notable absence, and Arthur Mann, a £30,000 signing from Notts County, the sole addition to a familiar Town line-up:

1. Ken Mulhearn
2. Jake King
3. Carleton Leonard
4. Graham Turner
5. Colin Griffin
6. Jack Keay
7. Trevor Birch
8. Ian Atkins
9. Dave Tong
10. Steve Biggins
11. Arthur Mann
12. Steve Cross

As Town's most experienced player, it was probably apt that Turner was featured in the 'Pro File' series for the first home league game. This season, though, it was a new sensation to see many more well-known players in the opposition teams. Reading their profiles in the programme, then watching them in the flesh, without doubt, enhanced the supporting experience for a teenage footy geek. County had Scottish international Don Masson ('spells with QPR and Derby County'), elegantly bossing the midfield, while Jeff Blockley ('a former England international') and Pedro Richards ('He likes nothing better than making long, overlapping runs up the right flank.' I wonder if they checked that with Pedro) were in defence to repel the Town forward line. In goal was Raddy Avramović ('a current Yugoslav international'), a club legend, who would contribute significantly to helping one of the founder members of the Football League reach the First Division in 1981. What a contrast to Notts County's fall from grace, and loss of league status in recent years.

My peak-geek years as a teenage football fan were probably 1977 to 1980. I devoured *Shoot!* and later *Match* every week, was obsessed with sticker albums and could name virtually every First Division team line-up at that time as well as the FA Cup Final teams from 1970 onwards. On a local level, I always bought the Town programme, wrote in the team changes (Maguire was crossed out and Birch written next to number 7 for this one), kept *Shropshire Star* cuttings and, oh what the heck, I can admit it now, even wrote my own mini report in a 'Matches I've been to' red Sterling exercise book. It was evident that I was no budding Brian Glanville, but the handwritten record does provide authentic documentation of the youthful enjoyment of following Town during that historic campaign. According to the brief entry for this fixture, the game was 'entertaining' and Trevor Christie opened the scoring for the visitors 'with a good header and then after a lot of pressure Salop equalised through Griffin'. Hardly Hugh

McIlvanney wordsmithery, and not quite doing justice to this important occasion, but at least covering the salient elements in what had essentially been a good performance. It was Shrewsbury Town's first point in the Second Division. We were up and running. Dead certs for relegation? Well, let's just see about that.

Home Matchday 2
'Don't bring me down'

After the triumphant highs of the previous season, this was beginning to look like a slightly inauspicious start to the new campaign, with so-called 'experts' sporting 'told-you-so' looks and even some of the local fans already writing the team off as doomed. In the programme for the next game away at Bristol Rovers, the section on Shrewsbury had led with the headline 'Division Two rookies make mixed start' and backed the statement up by mentioning the ousting of Halifax in the League Cup, the opening-day defeat at Swansea and the draw with Notts County. Aside from flagging up the bleedin' obvious, the programme did contain a more unusual feature as it listed the height and weight of each player next to the team line-ups. The first goal that day was scored by Rovers' shortest and lightest player, 5ft 7in, 9st Stewart Barrowclough, who converted a penalty past Town's heaviest player, 13st 11lb Ken Mulhearn.

The home team got a second goal before the referee that day, Clive Thomas of Porthcawl, blew his whistle again for another penalty, which Birch (height and weight not listed as it was a change to the published line-up) scored. In *Town Times* for the next league game at home to Cambridge United, 'Unlucky Shrewsbury' was the headline for the match report from Eastville after a 2-1 defeat. The doom-mongers now had a point, which was exactly what their local team had after three games. One point.

Conspicuous by its absence in the same edition, was the match report from the League Cup second round, first leg at Chesterfield played in midweek. Probably a simple decision for the editor – why draw attention to such a pathetic, crappy capitulation which Salop had lost 3-0? In his player-manager piece, Turner described how the opening games of the season 'have been a little disappointing as far as results go, although our performances have been quite pleasing'. He wasn't including the game at Saltergate which had been 'below par'. The return leg the following week was 0-0 and Town were eliminated. Reaching the second round had demonstrated some modicum of success though because since the dawn of the 1970s, Shrewsbury had crashed out in the first round on no less than seven previous occasions. Although this trend had undeniably demonstrated consistency, being consistently pants in the League Cup was far from ideal, especially with the knowledge that this was the club that had reached the semi-final of the competition on their debut appearance in 1961/62.

We were still without a win in the league, and Turner had emphasised that he felt 'no need for concern'. You could picture the boss giving a calm, motivational speech to the team in the dressing room, but you could also imagine, next to him, one of the more senior players (I'm going to go for Ken Mulhearn) taking on the Clive Dunn/Lance Corporal Jones role and ruining the pep talk by interrupting and excitedly shouting 'Don't panic, don't panic!' with his team-mates trying but failing to repress their giggles as their manager looks on stoney-faced. But maybe this *was* the day to get two points on the board and secure that first Second Division victory?

Over the last few seasons Cambridge United had soared dramatically from the Fourth Division to a very respectable 12th position in the Second Division in 1978/79. A tremendous achievement but they were still beatable, right? They only had one really well-known player, Alan Biley, who had made a name for himself for his free-scoring exploits and recognisable by his oh-so 1970s dodgy barnet. Ex-Norwich defender Dave Stringer certainly had experience but was in his mid-

30s. Okay, so they did have Tom Finney in the team too. Luckily, not that one – this one was the Northern Ireland international (so must have been half-decent too). Up to now, the U's had drawn their first three games, so it was clear Town weren't going to lose this one. Added to all this, Shrewsbury hadn't lost at home in the league since Ritchie Barker's first game in charge, that 3-2 defeat by Swindon on 25 February 1978 – an incredible run of 31 unbeaten matches. And today, key striker Steve Biggins was returning from injury after missing two games. What could possibly go wrong?

1 September 1979
Shrewsbury Town 1 Cambridge United 2
Attendance: 5,670

Disappointed! After 45 minutes, everything seemed to be going to plan. Town had been on top and the pressure was finally rewarded by a powerful header from our talismanic player-manager, Mr calmness personified, Graham Turner. No need to panic after all. The visitors had a couple of breaks but nothing much to worry about. Half-time, 1-0 Town, and everything under control. Our first win in the Second Division was 45 minutes away, but before breaking into a loud chorus of 'easy, easy' we had to see it out. And guess what? Second-half strikes from two not-very-well-known Cambridge players, Buckley and Spriggs (sounding more like a firm of solicitors rather than match-winning goalscorers), consigned Town to another loss and the termination of the undefeated home record. The entry in my teenage diary was predictably terse and perhaps a little hyperbolic: 'A disastrous game from Shrewsbury's point of view.'

Even the attendance was unsatisfactory. In the programme, a *Shropshire Star* reporter had said that any crowds under 5,000 would be 'disgraceful' and at this level a target of 8–10,000 should be 'comfortably realised'. The turnout was nearer to the lower figure for this game and if we were to get better crowds for the likes of West Ham, Sunderland et al, results would certainly need to improve. For sure, there was a solid fanbase at the club, with a whole new mini army of younger fans clutching their £12 junior season tickets (£12 – it seemed like a bargain even then!) but it's not much fun seeing your team lose every week, whoever you're playing.

The defeat was another setback, and the memories of cavorting deliriously on the Gay Meadow pitch, celebrating the championship after crushing Exeter 4-1 in May, seemed very distant. A quick scan down the Second Division at this time would reveal that Town were, in the words of Lynsey de Paul (and some bloke), rock bottom. So as the fans filed slowly out of the Wakeman End, the mood was markedly subdued. And with the next two fixtures away at Cardiff, then Chelsea at home, it looked as though it was going to be a lengthy, arduous winter. Oh well, to put an upbeat spin on it, at least we would be experiencing *one* season at this level.

Home Matchday 3
'Time for Action'

The Valley Motors bus gathered speed down the bank past Lydham Farm, slowing down to negotiate the sharp corner as it entered the village before drawing up next to a postbox embedded in the stone wall of the churchyard. Two teenagers wearing black Harrington jackets, straight-legged trousers and trainers embarked, heading for the game, their local club's first meeting with one of the big guns of the Second Division. The bus travelled along the A488, a quiet South Shropshire road, offering stunning views of Corndon Hill. Just beyond was Stapeley Hill, the location of Mitchell's Fold, a prehistoric stone circle and subject of local legend. Never mind stories involving an evil witch and a cow with special milk-producing powers, maybe later that very day, some humble men in striped shirts could perform their own brand of magic to overcome a bunch of powerful Giants from the South and thus create their own local legend.

The bus continued and was soon winding its way down the gloomy, slightly sinister Hope Valley, carefully negotiating the many twists and turns. Passing through Minsterley, the lads held their breath as long as possible to avoid the ghastly pong from the dairy. The bus meandered through Pontesbury and Hanwood, picking up a sprinkling of blue-and-amber-scarfed fans along the route. It descended the hill into Shrewsbury, past the Boathouse pub, with its admirable setting on a bend in the Severn opposite the Quarry, a picturesque park on the banks of the river. A few minutes later the bus crossed the Welsh Bridge and arrived in the town centre. The 20-mile journey had taken an hour.

From here, it was a brisk route march towards the ground, nipping down a side street on to Mardol, past the small amusement arcade with a constant racket blasting out from the space invader and fruit machines. It was a left turn at the Famous Army and Navy Stores on the corner, up Pride Hill then taking a right on to the High Street. No time to pop into Alltrees, the sports shop opposite Rackhams, or for a quick browse through the records in Durrants. No, today the teenagers were walking with purpose straight down the hill. In fact, oh my lads, you should have seen their faces, going down the Wyle Cop to see the Shrewsbury aces, all the lads and lasses, smiles upon their faces, going down the Wyle Cop, to seeeeee the Shrewsbury aces. Then they were striding over the English Bridge, the Gay Meadow stands and floodlights now firmly in their sights. Turning left into a narrow street, they joined the short queue outside the Wakeman End entrance, showed their £12 junior season tickets to the turnstile operator and rattled through into the ground on to the terraces before virtually sprinting towards the Riverside and plonking themselves on a metal barrier up near the buffet. It was just after 2pm, nearly an hour before kick-off. The lads were ready to live the dream.

In the programme for the previous match, away at Cardiff City, it was acknowledged that Shrewsbury were finding the transition to the higher level difficult, particularly when 'the first team squad is dominated by players of Third and Fourth Division backgrounds' (at least they hadn't said 'standards' instead of 'backgrounds', but you did wonder if that's what they really meant). In the next sentence though, Cardiff's writers paid tribute to their opponents (or was it damning with faint praise?) as 'a club of resilience and ambition led by one of the brightest young managers in football'. Unfortunately, this didn't do Town any good on the pitch and another narrow defeat ensued. After five league matches, the team were rooted to the bottom of the Second Division. A swift return to the nether regions of lower-league football looked inevitable. Make no bones about it, Shrewsbury's third home fixture of the season was massive. Despite the poor start, there was no doubting the fans' excitement for this game. The same couldn't be said for the local constabulary's perspective on the match. Chelsea were coming to town!

15 September 1979
Shrewsbury Town 3 Chelsea 0
Attendance: 9,271

Earlier that week, just to spice things up and blast anticipation levels into orbit, Chelsea's manager Danny Blanchflower had quit, leaving a former Telford boss in caretaker charge. The former gaffer of Town's neighbours also happened to be the hat-trick hero from England's 1966 World Cup-winning team – it was only Geoff Hurst! Oh, my word.

Fair play, this Chelsea team weren't a patch on the side that had won the FA Cup in the famous final against Leeds United at the start of the decade and the European Cup Winners' Cup the following year. There weren't any players that evoked that early 70s glamour as Peter Osgood, Alan Hudson and Peter Bonetti did. Nor was there a suitably monikered hard nut defender such as Ron 'Chopper' Harris. Their best player of the current era, Ray Wilkins, had moved to Manchester United in the summer. However, the talented left-winger Clive Walker had panache and was likely to be a threat (this threat was somewhat reduced when he was only named as a sub) and the 6ft 4in defender Micky Droy, a hybrid of James Bond's adversary Jaws and a yeti, was sure to be a fearsome opponent. The rest of the present line-up weren't household names, but decent footballers who would serve the London club well, such as Ray's brother Graham Wilkins, John Bumstead and Ian Britton. To pique even more interest in this first league meeting between the two sides, older Town fans hadn't forgotten the 3-2 defeat at Stamford Bridge in the fifth round of the FA Cup in 1966 in front of 51,000.

Chelsea had been relegated in May 1979, had started this campaign in distinctly average form and were now lying 11th in the table. Pre-season omens hadn't been good as they'd only won one of their friendlies, 3-1 against the People's Republic of China. This bizarre match-up conjured up memories of the TV footage of West Brom's tour of that country in 1978 and the moment when midfielder John Trewick was asked to comment on the Great Wall of China, which stretched majestically behind him, and said, 'When you've seen one wall, you've seen 'em all, haven't you?'

Back to that mid-September Saturday in 1979, and it was the reputation of some Chelsea fans that was the greatest concern for West Midlands police, so many of the travelling contingent were bussed from the station to the ground. It didn't prevent some skirmishes and my teenage match report stated that the game 'started off with trouble on the Riverside'. A euphemism for a bloody great scrap between mindless yobs.

After 12 minutes, the encounter on the pitch sprung to life too when Atkins' shot rebounded off Borota and Steve Biggins headed in, signalling that this might be a good day for Town, who were leading 1-0 at half-time with the home fans in good voice. The away hordes housed in the Station End were less vociferous now, but the simmering atmosphere felt more menacing. After the break, Shrewsbury's dominance increased and Arthur Mann volleyed in the second, his first goal for the club, and on 77 minutes Jack Keay clinched the win with a penalty. Predictably, the result didn't go down well with a sizeable portion of the away cohort who, keen to live up to their image, decided to rampage around a nearby housing estate, causing considerable damage. There were other sporadic outbreaks of meathead behaviour: one Chelsea fan was arrested for attempting to steal the match ball (always a tricky endeavour I find) and others had run amok in a local DIY store, sploshing paint everywhere including on themselves (not a great idea when it comes to proclaiming your innocence of involvement in any paint-sploshing incidents). I was oblivious to all this havoc though as I had an important mission to complete after the game.

A few years previously, as a Christmas present, I had been given a small rectangular book with a Japanese floral design on the front and back covers. Inside, the pages were blank and it was explained to me that the aim was to fill them with the signatures of other people. This gift triggered the beginning of an obsession with the ancient art of autograph collecting. I'd started slowly and domestically so the opening pages contained family members. I then moved on to friends followed by a PE teacher who also commented on a primary school football match he'd organised (15 November 74, Lydbury North 0 Bishop's Castle 13. Well done!) After that, I upped my game and objectives and we would wait patiently outside players' entrances before and after matches to secure the scrawled signatures of footballers, starting with the first batch of Shrewsbury stars: Hayes, Turner, Tarbuck, McGregor, King, Mulhearn, Haywood, Irvine, Durban, Kearney, Atkins, Maguire and Bates (whose name features three times – another hat-trick for Chico!)

The book also includes players from Newport County, Rotherham (Trevor Womble must have got some stick at that time), Halifax, Chesterfield and Peterborough. The first top-level players to feature were Wilf Smith and David Cross (Coventry City), harvested at a Wolves game. Later, a crop of top-of-the-range stars appear: John Richards, Mick Mills, Graeme Souness, Paul Madeley, Emlyn Hughes, Kevin Keegan, Brian Talbot as well as some *Star Soccer* presenters (Hugh Johns, Billy Wright and Trevor East). But it is the mixed bag of non-football names that makes this initial collection quite interesting: Lesley Judd (*Blue Peter*), Percy Thrower (the Shropshire gardener), Dave and Chris Baybutt, Gerald Short (grass track motorcyclists), Bryan Mosley (Alf Roberts in *Coronation Street*), Glenn Turner and Basil D'Oliveira (Worcestershire cricketers), Gayle Hunnicutt (American actress) and the *piece de resistance*, the one and only Bernard Bresslaw (*Carry On* films stalwart). Ludlow festival had provided some rich pickings, and also the guy who did stunts on *Z Cars.*

During this full-on autograph-collecting phase, I filled four and a half books, not only with the countless signatures of lower-league players (including Town players multiple times), but also with some of the starriest names in football over that period: there were bona fide legends (Norman Hunter, Billy Bremner, Liam Brady, Malcolm Macdonald, Trevor Francis, Denis Law and Bobby Charlton); managers (Jack Charlton, Bob Paisley, Ron Greenwood and Graham Taylor); men in black (Jack Taylor and Clive Thomas); commentators (Barry Davies, Archie Macpherson and Jimmy Hill); even the odd cult hero (Robin Friday of Reading). I was proud of my soccer signature treasure trove, but also pleased to have accumulated an assortment of various other bods who had put pen to paper for me: five members of Steeleye Span, Peter Townsend ('famous fighter pilot and close friend of Princess Margaret', but unfortunately not Pete, of The Who), Chris Bonnington, Jenny Pearson (British orienteering champion) and Tommy Cooper. I'd acquired the folk group's autographs after a concert at Wolverhampton Civic Hall. I have absolutely no recollection of where I obtained the others, but it must have been an interesting gathering.

I felt I had matured as a collector and needed to move to a higher level so was now seeking signatures on pictures cut out from football publications or on sticker cards. I'd upgraded to scrapbook format and had accrued signed pictures of Mick Channon, Andy Gray and a plethora of Norwich City players in that glorious green and yellow Admiral kit, including Kevin Reeves and the two Martins, Peters and Chivers.

The 1979/80 season was an opportunity to add to my hoard on a regular basis at a familiar location. I wasn't just going for the obvious, more famous players – I'd already got a few indecipherable scribblings on a Notts County team group photo after the opening home game – but some of the Chelsea cohort would be altogether bigger catches. So after the game, there I was waiting patiently outside the ground, hoping to ensnare my prey. The players took quite a while to emerge as they'd apparently been subjected to an angry rant from Geoff Hurst after their woeful performance (a dressing room dressing down?) I was happy to bag signed pics of Clive Walker, Ian Britton and Micky Droy and even happier to get Hurst's autograph, beside which I wrote 'Scorer of 3 goals in 1966 World Cup final', as a useful aide-memoire. But most of all, I was happy with the win. We were off the bottom.

At last Shrewsbury had been rewarded with a victory, and over one of the division's heavy hitters to boot! 'Two points in the sproutbag' in the local parlance. The *Shropshire Star*'s headline, 'Horror for Hurst as Town net first scalp', neatly captured the essence of some emergent county folklore, created by the 'Shrewsbury aces'.

Home Matchday 4
'Sail on'

The following fixture was at Charlton, who were now at the foot of the table without a win. The welcome pages of their match programme contained the customary gubbins that was being written about the Second Division newcomers. Town were described as 'the little Shropshire team with a big heart', a team with 'no stars', with players who 'are probably unknown outside the county' and whose success is built on 'team spirit and organisation'. A little patronising, a bit blunt, but not without some truth and at least the message about our 'little team' was essentially positive. Despite the euphoria of the Chelsea victory and all our 'little team' attributes, it all came to nothing on this occasion as Charlton broke their duck and won 2-1. This deposited Town back to the bottom of the league. Staying up in the Second Division was going to require very large hearts, an abundance of team spirit and top-notch organisation. And we had to hope that a few more creative skills would be added to the mix and on show soon.

The visitors for the fourth home match of the season were Orient, sitting one place above Shrewsbury in the table. Even at this early stage the game had the look of a relegation four-pointer (at only two points for a win, this phrase doesn't have quite the same ring). The mood was buoyant, though, as a fan favourite had re-joined 'Shrewsbury's happy family'– a phrase also used in the Charlton programme. Oh sod off, you condescending, (probably) dysfunctional metropolitan gits.

29 September 1979
Shrewsbury Town 1 Orient 0
Attendance: 6,176

Sammy Chapman had scored some vital goals in Shrewsbury's 1978/79 championship-winning season and cup run so was an important addition to the squad, particularly as Paul Maguire was still sidelined with a long-term injury. In the summer of 1979, the veteran ex-Nottingham Forest player, like many other professional footballers at the time, had travelled across the Atlantic in search of the American soccer dream by playing in the North American Soccer League (NASL). He hadn't joined one of the glamour teams such as New York Cosmos or LA Aztecs, but had gone on loan to the brilliantly named Tulsa Roughnecks, who were soon to play a friendly against Shrewsbury (more about this game later). 'The saga of Sammy', as *Town Times* described the transfer, had been protracted but now he had finally been given the go-ahead to play against the east London side.

There was another Town transfer tale (if not quite a saga) at that time: in his regular column, Turner had underlined the need for a 'recognised goalscorer' and was clearly frustrated that he hadn't been able to get a deal done for Aldershot's John Dungworth. The clear implication was that his front players urgently needed to, in a term borrowed from a more popular American sport, step up to the plate.

Orient were another opponent without a win so far but had drawn four, which meant they were a point above Town. Their experienced line-up included ex-West Ham pair Mervyn Day and Tommy Taylor, bearded striker Ian Moores and former England international – and legendary hairy-baldy – Ralph Coates (for other exemplars of this hairstyle, see also Bobby Charlton and Peter Noble of Burnley). This was never going to be easy. Or entertaining. Chapman was influential in the game and his experience stood out, yet it was a more unsung, but no less important player, who spotted an imaginary plate located around the six-yard box, stepped up to it and walloped in the winner.

Steve Biggins didn't appear to possess all the characteristics of an archetypal centre-forward. He wasn't particularly well-built or imposing in the air. He wasn't known for having silky ball control or a thunderous shot. If truth be told, he looked a bit gangly. And his hair was coiffured in suspiciously mullet-like fashion which made him resemble the keyboard player in a synth-pop band more than a professional footballer. The surname alone prompted titters. It could therefore be assumed that the striker did not inspire terror in opposition defences. But Biggins (and titter ye not) did possess one vital skill: he knew where the goal was when it mattered (on most occasions anyway). For this 15-year-old Town fan, and many other Shrewsbury supporters at the time, this combination of traits meant that Town's main front man acquired a certain cult hero status.

Joining the club from non-league Hednesford in 1977 and scoring 12 goals in the successful Third Division campaign, Biggins was an integral part of the first 11. In my player performance log of each game that I kept at the time (I wish I'd called it a 'playerometer' but sadly I didn't), the forward only merited a 6.5/10 in this vital bottom-of-the-table clash – it was Chapman, and Mulhearn, Keay and Griffin in defence who got the higher scores. Even 17-year-old debutant, Dean Edwards, drafted in as a strike partner for Biggins, got a 7/10, for his promising start. A Town career didn't pan out for this young player though and he went up north to Finland, grabbed a hatful, then returned to score more goals for Telford, Wolves, Exeter and Torquay. One that got away. Yet on that day, cometh the hour, well the 53rd minute at least, cometh our man Biggins to notch the crucial winner, firing past keeper Day. The *Shropshire Star* used the term 'goal ace' in its match report headline. It wasn't the only time in this inaugural season in the Second Division that the Shropshire supporters would hail the name of Steve Biggins.

My own review at the time was brief, 'Not a very good game but at least Salop got both points.' Sometimes you just have to grind them out. Shrewsbury had lived up to their reputation and demonstrated ample team spirit and organisation. Every player had contributed to this important win, but Sammy and Steve had made a particular impact, acknowledged by the fans at the game's close, before they all shuffled out of Gay Meadow on that late September day over 40 years ago.

Home Matchday 5
'One day at a time'

Town were appearing in the second tier of English football's pyramid for the first time and had moved above the relegation drop zone with two wins and a draw. Things were looking up. There were other side benefits of playing at this exalted level: there were more possibilities that your team would feature in football publications. The previous season, a four-page club spot in the *Marshall Cavendish Football Handbook* (part 19) had opened with the words, 'Are Shrewsbury Town for real?' The article highlighted that the club were at the right end of the Third Division but that the 'people of Shrewsbury don't seem convinced yet'. The piece detailed some of the promotion near-misses experienced by the impressive 1960s Town team managed by Arthur Rowley. It described how key players such as Ted Hemsley, Alf Wood, Frank Clarke and Peter Broadbent all played at higher grades.

There were colour photos of the 'goalscorers' (Maguire, Biggins and Atkins) relied upon to get Town up, as well as pics of Mulhearn and Turner ('midfield anchor, record buy, club coach and emergency manager'). Near the end of the coverage, outgoing boss Barker suggested, 'With the right manager, they might even break through this season … into the Second Division.' He was right. And the people of Shrewsbury had been convinced. And here we were – at the wrong end of the Second Division.

At this time, as well as getting local updates in the *Shropshire Star*, I would be getting a regular fix of all the other news that mattered through my subscription to *Shoot!*, the undisputed champion of football publications (though *Match* was just emerging as a possible contender). In late September 1979 a half-page article on Turner and Town appeared on page 43 of this esteemed magazine. What a moment. For years I'd scrutinised the previews, the reviews, the section on world football, 'News Desk', 'Ask the Expert', the 'Goal Lines' letters page. I'd check out the 'Football Funnies' cartoons, even though they didn't always live up to the title. I have to say I wasn't a big fan of 'You are the Ref' but the stunning black and white images did often grab my attention. The colour pictures were brilliant (and perfect for autograph signing), and I loved the 'Focus on' section especially as it revealed fascinating insights on the typically exotic lifestyle of a top footballer. For example, in the same 1979 edition containing the article on Shrewsbury, Frank McGarvey of Liverpool was in the spotlight and here are his responses (with my asides in italics):

Car: Alpine GL (*nice motor*)

Favourite food: prawns and good salads (*but not shite salads*)

Miscellaneous likes (*always an interesting category*): going to the races, playing golf and a good cabaret

Miscellaneous dislikes (*sometimes an even more interesting category*): waiting at airports *(Clearly a member of the International Jet Set)*

Favourite singers: The Drifters, Eagles, Rod Stewart, Leo Sayer and Bread (*like punk never happened*)

Biggest influence on career: Mr Ferguson (Aberdeen manager) at St Mirren (*good call, Frank*)

If you weren't a footballer, what do you think you'd be?: a joiner (*I didn't really know exactly what a joiner did apart from joining things, but it didn't sound very glamorous. But I guess from Frank's other answers, he was ok with the way things had turned out*)

I would also scour the adverts in *Shoot!*, wondering what to spend my hardly earned pocket money on. Naturally there was plenty of football gear I craved: boots by Dunlop, Puma, Gola and Power (including stud trimmers), Sportsmaster match balls, Uhlsport gloves endorsed by Jimmy Rimmer, or most appealing of all, Umbro replica kits (Arsenal, Watford and Clydebank were among the list of strips available; Shrewsbury wasn't). You could send off for all manner of club memorabilia: Soccercrest belts, scarves, badges (Spurs rule, olé), wall charts, calendars and pennants (Ruch Chorzow please. Sorry, sold out.) The games looked tempting – Logacta, Matchday or BoxBall soccer – or would it better to go for a budget option such as stamps or programmes?

At the time, I wasn't interested in 'Soccer record albums' but I have accumulated a few of these since. From the same company, there were also long lists of matches to order as 8mm home movies so you could 'relive great moments of soccer' on 200ft reels of film (silent or with sound) – Sweden 2 Yugoslavia 1, 1974 World Cup, anyone? And there were deluxe binders to keep your copies of *Shoot!* 'safe and tidy'. As a soccer-mad teenage kid, this was my sweetshop, but instead of Sherbet Fountains, Fizzers and Flying Saucers, I would lick my lips at the thought of a bargain bundle of Steve

Earl programmes, a pair of Gola Aztecs or, oh go on then, a Hajduk Split pennant please.

The article in *Shoot!* began with the headline 'Graham Turner has woken up sleepy Shrewsbury' and the piece described the upbeat mood at the club. As he did on a few occasions that season, the player-manager cajoled the fans to come and support the team, who were now appearing live, every week in the Second Division. Surely the visit of Leicester City, one of the promotion favourites, and the promise of a feisty Midlands derby, would attract a good crowd?

6 October 1979
Shrewsbury Town 2 Leicester City 2
Attendance: 9,045

To be honest, most Town fans didn't need much cajoling, particularly those teenagers brandishing £12 junior season tickets. We were well up for this one. Getting to Gay Meadow, however, wasn't a simple operation for quite a large proportion of local fans heading to home games. In the *Shoot!* piece the writer had referred to a 'sleepy little town', but for those living in the wild, outlying rural areas of South Shropshire, Shrewsbury almost seemed like a metropolis, and was wide awake with it. I went to school in Bishop's Castle but lived in Lydham – the village didn't even have a shop, let alone a pub. Sleepy? Just resting? Pushing up the daisies and dead, more like. The nearest 'supermarket' was Harry Tuffins, a few miles away in Churchstoke. Who knew that 40 years later this retail company would have its name emblazoned on the home shirt of the county's only Football League club? So on matchdays we would head to Shrewsbury to be entertained; for excitement, for thrills. This was where the action was. The expansive Shropshire catchment area is important for STFC though and there was always a decent, loyal turnout of supporters from this corner of the county (and still is).

My pithy but positive match summary at the time described the game as 'very exciting' with 'a good atmosphere' and Turner was probably quite pleased with the 9,000-plus attendance. Followers of both teams had many moments to shout about, with Sammy Chapman opening the scoring for Town from the trusted corner-header combination. Early in the second half Mark Goodwin drew the Foxes level with a brilliant 25-yard shot and the visitors took the lead in the 72nd minute with a goal from Byrne. But the Shropshire contingent were in good voice and when Jake King nodded in a well-deserved equaliser, the cheers rang out across the River Severn. The slumbering Salopians had certainly woken up now.

In the end, Turner was no doubt less happy with the result than his counterpart Jock Wallace, as Town were still failing to convert many of their chances into goals. The search for another forward would continue, particularly as some tough-looking games lay ahead – Notts County and Newcastle away, then a hotly anticipated home clash against local rivals Wrexham in two weeks' time. Despite the slight disappointment of not winning, it had been an impressive, encouraging performance against a strong outfit. The East Midlands team had a good blend of youth (Goodwin and Andy Peake) and experience (Dennis Rofe and keeper Mark Wallington) and would go on to become the Second Division champions later that season. It was probably a good job that Leicester didn't bring on their young substitute that October day, however. His name was Gary Lineker.

Home Matchday 6
'Dreaming'

Tulsa Roughnecks sounded as though they should have been on the starting grid for *Wacky Races*. Actually, they were a team from the burgeoning NASL who were soon to appear in a midweek friendly against Shrewsbury. But before that game, Town had a more important fixture against their arch-rivals from across the Welsh border. Forget the Birminghams, Chelseas and West Hams, Wrexham at home was going to be tasty.

20 October 1979
Shrewsbury Town 3 Wrexham 1
Attendance: 11,007

The previous two away matches had been a stark reminder that Shrewsbury were now playing at a higher level, and surviving in the Second Division was going to be a major challenge. In the programme for the first of those games, Notts County captain Brian Stubbs had outlined his concerns that his former colleagues, Sammy Chapman and Arthur Mann, might leave Meadow Lane with smiles on their faces in which case he would 'probably go away and shoot myself'. But Turner had already sold Mann (after a very short stay in Salop) to Mansfield and most of the shooting that night ended up with the ball in the back of the Town net. It was a 5-2 trouncing. Chapman wasn't smiling and neither were his team-mates. Stubbs was probably sporting a wry grin after the game, even though he scored an own goal. And it was 'nul' points from St James' Park too, Shrewsbury beaten 1-0 by Newcastle in front of a crowd of over 20,000. No shame in that as the Magpies were top of the league. But Town were now back in the relegation zone, with Burnley one place below. It was already clear that home form and the backing of local support was going to be vital.

For the Wrexham match, the *Town Times* programme provided a record of previous meetings between the near neighbours: it was neck and neck; both teams had won nine games and four had been drawn. The rivalry between the clubs had intensified over the years after numerous clashes in the Welsh Cup. Indeed, Town had beaten Wrexham in the two-legged final the season before – the icing on the cake of the championship-winning season. A sizeable turnout was drawn to Gay Meadow for this encounter, the first of five 10,000-plus home attendances over the season, with the majority of the crowd sensing that nothing short of a victory was required.

Wrexham were some side in those days, though, and in recent seasons they had claimed the scalps of many higher-level teams in cup competitions. In 1976 they had even reached the quarter-finals of the European Cup Winners' Cup before getting knocked out by Anderlecht, who went on to win the trophy that year.

Back to 1979 and the Welsh club had made a superb start to the season. Managed by former local star player Arfon Griffiths, Wrexham were sitting proudly in third place in the Second Division and starting to dream about promotion to the top table. Their team that day included Welsh internationals Dai Davies and John Roberts with deadly marksman Dixie McNeil up front.

Despite the quality and form of the opponents, it was Town who prevailed that day with the home centre-forward totally upstaging his more illustrious counterpart. Early on it was Steve Biggins who rose like a trout leaping from the Severn to head in the first goal. The striker made it two with a lob over Davies before substitute Whittle pulled one back for the visitors. In my teenage match report, I described how our number nine, about 20 minutes from the end, 'thundered in a volley to complete a brilliant hat-trick', Biggins' first in the league. Not bad for a former schoolteacher from Lichfield, who wasn't known for having a thunderous shot. Atkins, Tong and Wardle were also standout performers. The Riverside was rocking and three sides of the ground were lapping up a sweet victory, while for Wrexham, it was a rude awakening from the promotion dream and the initiation of a gradual slide down the table. Oh dear. How sad. Never mind.

Three days after that Second Division game, some Americans came to town. September and October 1979 was a popular time for NASL teams to go on tour – New York Cosmos, a kind of soccer equivalent of basketball exhibitionists Harlem Globetrotters, drew thousands to their games (even without Pelé, who had retired in 1977) in Hong Kong, Seoul, Jakarta, Singapore, Tokyo, Kuala Lumpur and Melbourne. After a short European tour, LA Aztecs came to the UK, and with Johan Cruyff in their team they were also an attractive proposition for their games at Birmingham and Chelsea.

And then there were Tulsa Roughnecks, who had played in Holland and Belgium in recent weeks, but now included Bangor, Worcester City and Shrewsbury on their busy schedule.

The itinerary really didn't seem to offer much rest time – the day before playing at the Meadow and the day after, the Roughnecks 'tied' games at Leicester City and Derby County respectively. The North American guests won the match squeezed in the middle, beating their Shropshire hosts. This rather peculiar match-up, remarkably, was probably still not the oddest in the club's recent history of friendlies against unlikely opponents, which also included a 'public practice match' against a Saudi Arabia XI in 1976. That honour surely went to Zambia, the occasion notable for featuring one of the most famous players to ever pull on a Shrewsbury Town shirt, even more well-known than Arthur Rowley, Alf Wood and a few years later, Derek Smalls (in *This is Spinal Tap*). For this was the game in which Bobby Charlton, 1966 England World Cup hero, donned the club jersey. And which footballing legend do you think appeared on the front cover of the match programme that day? Well, it was none other than Town stalwart Jimmy Lindsay.

Salop won 4-0 and in my review of the game I took great pleasure in penning the words 'Bobby Charlton played well for Shrewsbury'. Can't remember much about Jimmy Lindsay's performance but I'm sure he did fine. Even though he would have been 42 years old, Town could have done with Bobby Charlton in midfield for the following game at Birmingham.

Home Matchday 7
'Star'

It was early November 1979 and Shrewsbury were still finding their feet in the Second Division. The two-page spread in the *Birmingham City News* programme before the next game at St Andrew's offered a few more nuggety insights than the usual bland guff about the away team. It noted that this was not the first time Town had played a competitive league game in the city (not counting the Birmingham League up to 1937) having appeared twice at Villa Park in the early 1970s. In this first league match against the Brummie Blues, the home team won 1-0, making it the seventh successive away game Town had lost, leaving them second from bottom. It really wasn't looking good and yet another difficult prospect lay just around the next corner. The team had already played all three Welsh clubs in this division, beating Wrexham convincingly in the last home game but losing at Ninian Park and Vetch Field. Next up was the return against Swansea City.

3 November 1979
Shrewsbury Town 2 Swansea City 2
Attendance: 9,815

Going to an away game took your fandom to another level. Following your team to distant stadiums in unfamiliar, enemy territory offered exciting, novel experiences. I liked to think that these forays beyond the county borders opened your eyes to pastures new (Turf Moor), broadened your mind by travelling to outlandish locations (the Wirral peninsula), provided unforgettable moments and a tale to tell, perhaps a (mental) scar to show (coming right up). Your kudos as a hardcore supporter amongst your school-mates increased. Well, that's how it felt to a teenage Salop fan after an away day.

A trip to Swansea late in the previous season had certainly been memorable, but the off-the-pitch events that night weren't exactly fun or edifying. Shrewsbury had earned a point in a competitive 1-1 draw against a promotion rival and the away cohort were in fine fettle as we began the trip back to Shropshire. Somewhat unwisely the coach driver decided to draw up at a chip shop on the outskirts of the city, and that's when it got a bit unpleasant. After stopping, a small posse of

Swansea fans immediately boarded our vehicle, with little opportunity for the Salopian passengers to repel this sudden incursion. They were led by a tall, wiry, lank-haired hard case who pronounced that he wanted a Town scarf as a 'souvenir'. Any potential resistance was ruled out when someone muttered that the intruder had a knife, and it all went a bit quiet. The greasy-haired thug strode to the back of the coach and acquired his trophy. As the boarding party headed back down the aisle, a couple of our fans were casually thumped, including my mate's older brother who couldn't help blurting out, 'I only came to watch a football match.' Even at this rather scary moment, the comment provoked some involuntary, but very quiet, sniggering. But most of us took the safer option of keeping schtum, cowered in our seats, hoping we weren't going to get a fairly random smack in the face by this clearly deranged Welsh loon. As we pulled away from the chippy, the local nutter held his prize aloft, grinned maniacally and gave us a cheery V sign. Nobody waved back. After that, the mood on the journey home was slightly more subdued.

With former Liverpool legend John Toshack at the helm, the Swans had risen from the fourth to the second tier in consecutive seasons and in the following campaign would gain promotion to the top division for the first time. In late 1979, Swansea were comfortably positioned in mid-table and their team contained some vastly experienced, quality players such as Tommy Craig, John Mahoney and Ian Callaghan. Rising, talented younger stars such as Robbie James and Jeremy Charles could play a bit too. Thankfully, ex-Liverpool defender Tommy Smith, the 'Anfield Iron', had just announced his retirement but this was still going to be yet another tough encounter.

Town had recently received some positive news though, with the long-awaited return of key player Paul Maguire after injury, and there he was on the cover of *Town Times*. The Scottish winger had been the top scorer in the title-winning season and had also contributed many assists from set pieces. All the players who starred in 1978/79 are club legends in my eyes but he was undoubtedly my favourite. The ruddy-cheeked star even had his own simple, but distinctive chant, 'Maguire, Maguire, Maguire, der-der, der-der, der-der.' Years later, I got the t-shirt. A further boost had also been provided by the club record signing of striker John Dungworth from Aldershot for £75,000 plus a further £25,000 after he had played 30 games. Perhaps these two players would make a difference to the team's form.

On the day it was the Welsh side who went in front before the debutant Dungworth headed in to make it

1-1. A 30-yard screamer from Craig looked to have sealed a victory for the visitors when, deep into stoppage time, a Swansea defender handled in the box – penalty! And up stepped Jack Keay to level from the spot. While the home supporters celebrated, Toshack castigated the ref for his timekeeping. The away contingent, players and manager looked utterly gutted to concede such a late equaliser, but for those Town fans who had been on that coach to Swansea the previous season, this denouement was really rather pleasing.

Home Matchday 8
'Knocked it off'

In the glorious Third Division championship-winning campaign of 1978/79, Watford had been Shrewsbury's closest rivals in the race for promotion and the title. In April, an impressive crowd of over 13,000 had piled into Gay Meadow to watch a slightly anti-climactic 1-1 draw. Some Town fans had amused themselves by baiting the packed away fans in the Station End with unsavoury chants about Elton John, their club chairman. If they had been berating the artist formerly known as Reg Dwight for the deterioration of his musical output since that magnificent early 1970s period, that would be have been one thing, but regrettably, that wasn't the general theme of the chanting. These were not enlightened times.

Watford were eventually pipped for the title by one point, but in Graham Taylor they had an inspirational young manager who had led the Hornets from the Fourth Division to the Second Division in successive seasons and would take them to the top level for the first time in 1982. Back in the autumn of 1979, Shrewsbury had edged out of the bottom two but really needed to beat Watford this time.

10 November 1979
Shrewsbury Town 1 Watford 0
Attendance: 8,150

Unlike the previous season, both clubs were at the wrong end of the table so a lower attendance than that five-figure total would be understandable. Town were now getting decent turnouts for home fixtures and supporters could see that the team were fighting bravely for their survival in the second tier. The team had put in some solid performances, even though results hadn't always gone well. For this teenage fan, knowing that there would be a decent atmosphere and a sizeable away contingent certainly added to the anticipation and the thrill of the games. In contrast, just five years earlier, down in the Fourth Division, that anticipation would have been tinged with some trepidation as I headed off to watch Town against, say, Hartlepool. Away fans and thrills had been in much shorter supply back then so we were fully aware that this new-fangled high life needed to be embraced and savoured.

The recent promotion battle had generated some rivalry with Watford, but this was nothing compared to that shown between local junior football teams. In my experience, the competitiveness started early with games against nearby schools – who can honestly forget Bishop's Castle Primary's 13-0 drubbing of Lydbury North on their patch? Then at secondary level, there were hard-fought tussles against Craven Arms or Tenbury Wells. If my dad came to watch one of the games he would stand on the touchline, bring his hands together and implore us to 'face up'. That phrase may have been acceptable in the Midland League in the late 1940s, but when it was uttered now, it provoked bemused looks from team-mates as we chased the ball around the playing field. Why couldn't he just yell, 'Get stuck in, Castle,' like the other dads? I know it was well-meant encouragement, but it did feel a little embarrassing at the time.

There were giant-killings too – in the school four-a-side tournament, we entered the sports hall as ticker tape rained down from the balcony, a habit picked up from the 1978 World Cup footage. As underdogs, this spurred us on to outplay a team two years above us, knocking them out and then getting congratulated by burly, older lads who shook our hands and patted our backs, overjoyed at seeing their peers humiliated. In an inter-school five-a-side competition, we beat the hotly fancied hosts Pontesbury on penalties (I missed mine) to cap an enjoyable, rewarding evening. We got medals!

I didn't have quite the same affinity for other sports such as cricket or rugby, but it was a small school so if you showed any capacity to kick, catch, throw or handle any sort of ball-type object (small, round and leathery, bigger, round and leathery or oval and leathery), then you were in. I was not alone in finding rugby rough, boorish and quite scary, particularly when you got picked as full-back. On one occasion playing away at Church Stretton, when our rugby-preferring PE teacher blew the whistle to start the game, terrified, we all shrieked 'chaaaaarge' at the top of our pre-pubescent voices and headed valiantly to meet our doom, like a modern-day mini sporting Light Brigade. Mr Martin, our PE teacher, did not see it that way and, not amused, called us back, told us off and restarted the game. Stretton's not-so-secret weapon was a large lad known as 'Spanner'. His team-mates simply fed him the ball and he ripped through our ranks. I have no idea how many tries he scored that day, but it was a lot. My chum, Griff and I didn't really care though as we'd been substituted at half-time, relieved that our bodies were still generally intact – our mates' envy was palpable as they watched us prance joyfully towards the changing rooms.

Apart from school rivalries there were other competitors on the scene. I played for a Bishop's Castle junior side. We ran out and around in a lovely, orange-topped kit with two stripes down the side of the shirts. Far nicer than the black-and-white-striped jerseys worn by Magpies, a team based in Church Stretton which attracted and lured players, not just from that town, but also from other local areas (except that they didn't always get the best ones, mind). I hated Magpies. My loathing was not just contained to the pitch. Magpies had links with teams in Holland so went on football tours there. That wasn't fair. Our team hadn't even had a trip to Borth.

The fact that some of the parents went on those excursions did lead to some ridicule though. A mate who played for them later told me that as their team coach passed through the red light district of Amsterdam, the lads were told by the mums to avert their eyes and look the other way. I bet some of them did, too. What a bunch of wussies. On one occasion, it was very satisfying to be part of the Castle team that totally outclassed those upstarts, including my long-haired school buddy Griff, by winning 12-5. Result. You can stick your tulips where the sun don't shine. There was stiffer competition in other parts of Shropshire, though, from the likes of Up and Comers, Column Colts and Saints. These were well-drilled, talented young teams that took their junior football very seriously. We didn't get much change against that lot. Playing for Bishop's Castle Juniors in this league seemed to parallel the challenges that Shrewsbury would later face in the 1979/80 season: we were a less-heralded, small-town team, with fewer individual stars, on fewer resources in a league full of big shots. It was tough but we adjusted to the situation. I once scored a stunning half-volley against Colts at their place and remember our management team staring at me with incredulity after the ball had flown into the top-right corner. It was a rare moment of personal skill, but we still got hammered.

Six years on from watching my first Shrewsbury game, Town dominated the match against Watford but struggled to break down the away team's solid defence. However, in the 66th minute, the pressure paid off when a Maguire effort heading for goal was handled by Harrison. For the second home game in a row, 19-year-old Scottish centre-back Jack Keay calmly converted the penalty. In goal for Town that day, as he had been at my Gay Meadow debut back in 1973, was Ken Mulhearn. The former Manchester City keeper joined Shrewsbury in 1971 and made over 400 appearances, securing 'official legend' status. He was a very popular figure at the club and after he passed away in 2018, hundreds attended his funeral at a local church. In that game against Watford, Mulhearn made a couple of vital saves in the closing stages, earning my man of the match accolade with a commendable eight out of ten. We were fortunate to have a player of such class – our keeper had been a key part of the title-winning City team of 1968. Town held on for a 1-0 victory.

The comments in my match report weren't exactly complimentary though, 'An uninteresting game … Salop weren't very good.' So what? It really didn't matter. Shrewsbury had ground out the win and were able to leapfrog their opponents in the league standings. Up the table we must go, ee-aye, ee-aye, ee-aye, oh.

* * *

FA Cup Interlude 1

In this book I've been recounting the memorable 1979/80 campaign, Shrewsbury Town's first season in the old Second Division. Playing at such a high level meant another first for the club – Town would not enter the FA Cup until the third round in January. These interludes will focus on Shrewsbury's FA Cup fortunes in the 1970s.

23 November 1976
FA Cup first round replay
Shrewsbury Town 4 Doncaster Rovers 3
Attendance: 6,234

It's not really the early round encounters that first grab the attention of young fans, but the cup finals that make the indelible impressions on adolescent imaginations. And it wasn't just the matches – the TV build-up on *Grandstand* or *World of Sport* from late morning onwards was part of that experience. *The Road to the Final*, *Cup Final It's a Knockout!* or simply seeing the players interviewed in hotels or on coaches en route to the stadium were all essential viewing for young football supporters.

My first memory of a final is 1971, which featured Charlie George's iconic 'lying down' goal celebration (basically, he was knackered). The year after it was Allan 'Sniffer' Clarke's diving header. Get in! Like millions of other viewers, I couldn't believe Jim Montgomery's double save which helped Sunderland win the FA Cup in 1973. Kevin Keegan and Liverpool easily beat Newcastle a year later with Malcolm 'Supermac' Macdonald ballooning his best chance high into the Wembley sky. In 1975 Alan Taylor became a West Ham legend by getting both goals in their win against Fulham, while Bobby Stokes and Roger Osborne gained immortality in the eyes of Southampton and Ipswich fans by netting the winners in '76 and '78 respectively. Manchester United's 2-1 victory in 1977 prevented Liverpool from becoming the first team to win the treble. In 1979 it was the ecstasy etched on Alan Sunderland's face after scoring the last-gasp winner against the Red Devils which encapsulated the high drama of English football's showpiece event. Each time, after the trophy had been presented, after hours spent glued to the telly, it was straight outside for a kick-about. Over 40 years on, all these FA Cup memories are still firmly embedded in my mind – I didn't even need to check t'internet for the details.

For lower league and non-league teams, though, the excitement kicks off in the first round. Most football supporters have a good geographical awareness of the location of league teams and for younger fans back in the 1970s, this knowledge was often gleaned from the *Bartholomew Football History Map of England and Wales*. When the minnows enter the competition, some destinations may be a bit more obscure. Shrewsbury faced their fair share of non-league opposition in the FA Cup first round in this decade, kicking off on the Somerset coast in 1970 when they avoided an upset by beating Minehead 2-1 with Geoff Andrews getting the winner. Two years later, Spennymoor were pulled out of the hat and this away trip may have had fans rooting around in atlases or on maps. Again, Town's blushes were spared with Peter Dolby scoring in a 1-1 draw. Back at Gay Meadow, the plucky team from the north-east were dispatched 3-1. In 1974/75, the first round threw up a home tie against Northern Premier League outfit Wigan Athletic, a strong team at that level and managed by future Town boss Ian McNeil. Sure enough, they got a 1-1 draw then knocked Shrewsbury out in the replay in front of over 11,000. Little did anyone know that much later the Latics would go on to win the ultimate prize.

After seeing the first-round draw the following season, Shrewsbury fans were probably asking the question 'Where on earth is Rossendale?' Their opponents turned out to be a semi-professional team based in a village in Lancashire. Town narrowly side-stepped this banana skin as Chic Bates bagged the only goal. Phew.

Shrewsbury had mixed first-round fortunes against league teams in the 1970s, beating Colchester, Mansfield and Doncaster (twice) but losing to Wrexham. I was at the 4-3 replay win against Doncaster in 1976 which I summarised in my teenage match report, 'A cracking game. Paul Maguire was ace. He scored three and made the fourth.' I had experienced my first taste of FA Cup magic, an appetising starter before the 1978/79 feast which I will be happy to serve up later.

Home Matchday 9
'I just can't be happy today'

In the QPR programme for the game in mid-November, Tony Pullein ('The League's top Feature Writer') provided a helpful reminder that Town were the only team in the division without an away point and that it had been a 'very tough initiation for Shrewsbury in this class of football and they are now in serious danger of making a quick return to the Third Division'. Cheers, Tone. The journalist did go on to say that the team had 'the ability to play themselves out of trouble' and that they would be 'stiff opposition' for the Loftus Road hosts. Not stiff enough though as Town went down to a late goal, their eighth away defeat on the trot. The danger signs were now flashing.

The following week, however, the team dusted themselves down after this disappointment, travelled up to Boundary Park, produced a solid performance and earned a 2-0 victory over Oldham courtesy of a Maguire brace. This good news was unexpected and coming two days before my 16th birthday, the two points were a welcome early gift. In his column for the programme, Graham Turner unsurprisingly hoped that the win would be 'the turning point and we can string a few results together and begin to move up the table'. Well, that went well.

1 December 1979
Shrewsbury Town 1 Luton Town 2
Attendance: 8,559

In the two previous home games, Shrewsbury had entertained upwardly mobile clubs in the shape of Swansea and Watford, and Luton were the third to fall into that category. Under the stewardship of David Pleat, who incidentally made a few appearances for Town in the late 1960s, the team were riding high in the Second Division and would go on to become champions in 1982. They had some classy young players such as defender Mal Donaghy, midfielder Ricky Hill and exciting forward Brian Stein. It goes without saying (but let's say it to reiterate the relentlessly daunting nature of the opponents faced that season), that this would be another difficult contest for Town.

Possibly in the hope of frightening these talented adversaries, adorning the front cover of *Town Times* for this game was Steve Hayes, sporting a fine set of mutton chops and looking like a cross between a petty hoodlum in *The Sweeney* and the drummer in a hard rock band (both good things of course!) With his long hair flowing, Hayes would chase down, and when necessary, scythe down opposing players. Step-overs may not have been his forte, but home supporters would marvel at his agricultural challenges. What

Hayes lacked in finesse, he more than made up for in passion and aggression. Watching him in full flow hurtling down the right flank towards the opposition defence was captivating. You could almost imagine him as a hairy, very wild ancient Briton, clad only in a loincloth (rather than blue and amber kit) and tearing towards an anxious legionnaire, who wasn't feeling very comfortable at being positioned at left-back on hostile, enemy soil. Thankfully, the outcome wasn't always quite as messy as expected.

Back in 1978, Hayes had been one of a small band of Shrewsbury players who had been selected for the *Sun Soccercards* series, essentially badly drawn football men depicted on cards. Due to a cock-up at the printing press, our Jake's image got mixed up with a J. (Jeff) King of Walsall. Apart from that, the Town representatives got off quite lightly – you should check out some of the other images, which border on the grotesque. On the back of Hayes's card, the defender was described as 'hard tackling', which was quite an understatement. To some Gay Meadow regulars, the full-back was known as 'Hannibal', while others fondly remember him as Steve 'Animal' Hayes. Either way, he must have been a scary proposition for opponents.

As it turned out, although Hayes had been a reliable squad player for the previous few seasons, he didn't play in the Luton game and only made five appearances in 1979/80. The likes of Stein and other skilful attacking players at this level can count themselves lucky not to have met Town's most uncompromising defender or heard the Riverside chant of 'Six foot two, eyes of blue, big Steve Hayes is after you' as he roared towards his unfortunate prey.

For the first third of the game against the Hatters, Shrewsbury were dominant with Jack Keay belting in the opener after 30 minutes. After that the tide turned and Luton showed off their offensive prowess. Stein equalised four minutes later and soon after that it was the veteran former Birmingham City and Blackpool striker Bob Hatton who poached the second, and ultimately winning, goal. Town switched off, were punished and didn't recover. In my teenage match report, I stated that 'the match was a little bit of a disappointment' but this probably didn't quite capture the mood of despondency felt by Turner, his players and a large proportion of the 8,500 crowd. It was a backward step after the victory at Oldham. Getting a result at fellow strugglers Fulham in the following game was looking even more important now, particularly as the next visitors to the Meadow would be West Ham.

* * *

FA Cup Interlude 2

So how did Shrewsbury fare in the FA Cup second round in the 1970s? When it comes to this stage of the competition, the anticipation increases as clubs scent potential glory and untold wealth and fame, knowing that getting over this hurdle could mean a trip to Old Trafford, Anfield or at least a home tie against mid-table First Division opposition.

13 December 1975
FA Cup second round
Shrewsbury Town 3 Chester City 1
Attendance: 6,061

Town's FA Cup ventures in the first half of that decade were not exactly dazzling. The team failed to get past the first round on two occasions and also lost to Reading and Bolton at the next stage. The only second-round success in this period was a home victory against that crack outfit from the footballing hotbed of Surrey, Guildford City, in 1971. However, from 1975 to the end of the decade, there was a notable upward trend in Salop's cup performances. Town's second-round opponents in this period were all teams north of Shrewsbury and on each occasion, the hurdle was successfully negotiated with wins over Chester City, Bury, Stockport County and Doncaster Rovers. In 1979/80, playing in the

Second Division, meant that Town didn't enter until round three. My first experience of the FA Cup was that second-round tie against local rivals Chester, and it didn't disappoint.

Leading the line that day were Ray Haywood and Phil Bates, two strikers signed from Stourbridge in 1974 for £10,000. Whether it was a 'buy one (striker), get one free' offer is not known. But what is clear, is that it was an astute piece of business by manager Alan Durban, as by the end of 1974/75, the duo had netted 38 goals between them with Town surging to promotion, finishing as runners-up to champions Mansfield.

Phil was better known to supporters as 'Chic' Bates, and his consistency, tireless running and goals at this time marked the beginning of a long-standing relationship with Shrewsbury. After leaving to play for Swindon Town and Bristol Rovers, Chic returned to the club in the early 1980s, becoming the manager in 1984 and steering his charges to equal the club's record league finish of eighth in the Second Division in 1985 (Turner's team had set this high bar in 83/84). Later he was deservedly inducted in the club hall of fame. He also got a name check on a Half Man Half Biscuit track ('Four Skinny Indie Kids', if you're interested). Respect. In 1977/78, to commemorate his 100th appearance, Chic appeared in the 'Focus on' section of *Town Times* and it was revealed that he drove a Cortina estate, enjoyed steak and chips and *The Two Ronnies* and that his ambition was to meet Muhammad Ali, but 'not in the ring'. Nothing remarkable (for the time), and that's probably what Town fans loved most about Chic Bates – he wasn't a particularly remarkable player and may not have possessed the skills of Sammy Irvine or the flair of Alex McGregor, but he certainly put in a shift and was often on hand to bag a goal or two. He was a proper Town hero for many.

In that second-round game against Chester back in 1975, I had just turned 12 and in my exercise book I described the encounter as 'a very good match but it was very cold'. Despite wearing a de rigueur green parka (like the one worn by those teeny hordes swarming on to the pitch after Ronnie Radford's stunner for Hereford against Newcastle a few years earlier), the coat does not seem to have been that effective, weather-wise. Town were in good form and it is highly likely that the strains of a popular little ditty rang out across Gay Meadow that day, 'Chic, Chic, Chic, Chic, Chico, score a little goal for me. Chic, Chic, Chic, Chic, Chico, I want one, two or three.' Chic, Chic, Chico was happy to oblige and netted twice in a 3-1 victory.

The man who had originally signed Bates for Shrewsbury, Alan Durban, notched the other. Nice.

So Town were now in the hat for the third round of the FA Cup – what glory and fame awaited? Manchester United or Liverpool away? Nope. It was a home tie against Fourth Division Bradford. We lost 2-1. But fear not, cup glory beckoned.

* * *

Home Matchday 10
'Walking on the moon'

I couldn't wait to tuck in to the next delicacy on the menu. This is why I'd bought a junior season ticket for £12. Shrewsbury's upcoming home game was against West Ham United. In a Second Division fixture. Town would be playing a team who had not only lifted the FA Cup twice (the last time just four years ago!), but had also won a European Cup Winners' Cup final. Brooking, Bonds and co. were on their way to Gay Meadow. Awesome! The imminent arrival of the Inter-City Firm, the notorious travelling group of West Ham fans, was slightly more troubling. I figured that this infamous mob probably wouldn't be interested in the Valley Motors Bus Service Crew from Bishop's Castle, but as this elite Salopian force never existed, we didn't really need to worry. As for the prospect of the game itself, oh maaaaan, I was counting down the minutes until kick-off.

15 December 1979
Shrewsbury Town 3 West Ham 0
Attendance: 8,513

I'd encountered my favourite Hammer person twice before when he had appeared as one of the 'Soccer Super Stars' at Plas Madoc Leisure Centre, near Wrexham. A few years previously, my parents had driven a bunch of us over to attend two of these day-long events in the summer when well-known footballers gave training sessions for groups of star-struck youngsters. You could hone your passing with Trevor Brooking, improve your shooting with Kevin Keegan, develop your tackling with Emlyn Hughes, work on heading with John Toshack or practise shot-stopping with Ray Clemence. Also on hand were Mike Smith, the Wales manager, and other internationals such as Dennis Tueart, Terry Yorath and Brian Greenhoff.

It was an incredible feeling to kick balls about with these superstars, who were not only sharing their skills but were also happy to pose for photos and sign autographs. Keegan was the centre of attention, charming everyone (particularly the mums, it seemed), but for us it was Brooking, looking splendid in a Wales track top, whose warm, affable personality made the biggest impact. Such close contact with all these soccer heroes really felt like footballing heaven for me, my brother and our friends.

Town Times on that mid-December afternoon in 1979 had a great photo of Ted Hemsley leading out Shrewsbury in a friendly against the Hammers in 1967. To his left was Bobby Moore, followed by Martin Peters, each holding a brown leather ball. Both players had been World Cup winners for England the previous year. The game in 1979 would be the first league meeting between the two sides. Admittedly, West Ham weren't the vintage team of yore and this was their second season at this level, but Trevor Brooking, Billy Bonds, Phil Parkes, Frank Lampard and Stuart Pearson were highly experienced, quality First Division campaigners. Their team also contained talented younger players such as Alvin Martin, Geoff Pike and Paul Allen, all destined for long careers at the top level too. Perhaps their most gifted player, Alan Devonshire, was injured. The east London club lay seventh in the table. Town had lost their previous two games, at home to Luton and away at Fulham (2-1), and this was certain to be yet another tough contest.

Or was it? Brooking's elegant midfield play represented the West Ham style. Bonds, Lampard and Martin were resolute defenders and Pearson, the former Manchester United striker, spelt danger up front. But Town had Ian Atkins, and on the day, the East Enders couldn't match the gritty determination, hard work and flashes of brilliance that 'Acker' and his team-mates produced to run out worthy winners.

Atkins was our 'Captain Marvel', the driving force in the team, an inspiration to those around him. He tackled hard, ran incessantly, passed well and scored his fair share. With his jet-black hair and 'tache, he cut a dashing figure, a cross between Burt Reynolds and a musketeer. We all loved Ian Atkins. It was no great surprise that he was snapped up by First Division Sunderland in 1982 and later went on to play for Everton, Ipswich and Birmingham.

One of Town's less acclaimed squad members also put in a solid midfield performance that day alongside Atkins. Jimmy Lindsay was a seasoned pro and had actually started his league career for West Ham. The Scot was one of those players who fans don't notice (or even appreciate) much, one of the guys who *won't* be spraying 40-yard 'Hollywood' balls across the park or attempting audacious overhead scissor kicks from outside the box with their 'wrong' foot; these fellows are more likely to break up play unobtrusively with a timely tackle or make themselves available as an outlet, before executing a low-risk pass to one of the more creative distributors in the side. Such players are often unassuming, seemingly functioning below the radar, but are nonetheless vital cogs in the team machine. Lindsay had one of these roles and was an important player during the club's successful period, making 86 appearances for Town but scoring only one goal (away at Stockport in the cup). See what I mean?

Although it was a disappointing crowd against West Ham, it was certainly a memorable day for the home fans present. Maguire opened Town's account, Chapman added a second with an audacious overhead kick (in contrast to Jimmy Lindsay, always available to assume the 'showman' role) and in the 85th minute, there was Acker to volley in a brilliant third. Course he was. Legend.

A few Hammers players were magnanimous enough in defeat to sign my Topps football cards after the game. My old acquaintance Uncle Trev (as he is affectionately known in my circle of close friends) was one of those who naturally obliged. Brooking would go on to score a headed winner against Arsenal in the 1980 FA Cup Final just a few months hence – a deserved success for such a great player and thoroughly decent bloke. Also, in the programme that December day was a competition to win a Chukie turkey from the well-known local company based in Craven Arms. Sod the poultry prize (if you'll pardon the expression), our Christmas present had come early as Town had stuffed those West Ham turkeys in a league fixture, well and truly bursting those famous bubbles. The ICF would not be zipping back to the metropolis on the high-speed rail network but would be on the slow train to Wolverhampton calling at Oakengates, Shifnal and Cosford, with ample time to mull over the day they got spanked by a small team from Shropshire.

Bobby Moore, Martin Peters, Geoff Hurst, Ron Greenwood, Alf Garnett, Billy Bonds, can you hear me? Billy Bonds, your boys took a hell of a beating! Your boys took a hell of a beating!

Home Matchday 11
'Wonderful Christmastime'

On Boxing Day 1979, Town travelled up to Preston and lost 3-0. That must have been grim. If it was any consolation for the Shrewsbury fans (and players for that matter) returning from that fruitless trip up north, ITV was dishing up a televisual feast of comedy that evening: *The Dick Emery Special* followed by *Man About the House*. BBC1 was offering *Where Eagles Dare* and on BBC2 it was ballet followed by Willy Russell's *Our Day Out*. But that was your lot in terms of TV channels.

After also losing at Sunderland a few days earlier, we weren't exactly having a fizzing wonderful Christmastime. Still, at least we now had a home fixture in the festive period to look forward to. It was only halfway through the season, but the game against lowly Bristol Rovers had 'vital clash between potential relegation candidates if they don't improve their form sharpish' written all over it.

29 December 1979
Shrewsbury Town 3 Bristol Rovers 1
Attendance: 7,097

While loyal (Masochistic? Foolish? Inebriated?) Town fans were experiencing a cold, miserable time on the terraces at Deepdale on the last Boxing Day of the 1970s, I was probably out playing football or riding around on my racer (I'd missed the boat with Raleigh Choppers earlier in the decade and anyway, they looked terribly uncomfortable), then later sharing a large bottle of Woodpecker or Bulmers cider with mates. Way back then, Christmas usually yielded some footy-related gifts – a silk scarf, a diary, maybe a keyring? Most of this tat was gratefully received then shoved in a drawer. One mug (with 'Come on you Blues' on the back) and a wooden door hanger thing looked as though they had been produced in the 1950s. At least I didn't ever get a rattle or a rosette.

At that game with Rovers, I'm sure a few festive tunes were played over the tannoy. It's also probable that the Christmas number one was played, Pink Floyd's distinctly un-Christmassy 'Another Brick in the Wall'. I wasn't interested in that tosh. In late 1979, I was more likely to be listening to a home-taped recording of *John Peel's Festive 50*. That year, Stiff Little Fingers, The Jam and The Undertones were all in the top ten of this chart. Now, that's what I call decent music. At Gay Meadow, they certainly weren't going to be playing any PiL, but it was always uplifting for Town fans to hear the jaunty sounds of The Dave Clark Five's 'Catch Us If You Can' (mmmm-mm-mm) blaring out, as the players ran on to the pitch.

Although Shrewsbury's away form had been shocking with 11 defeats out of 12 games, apart from the odd blip, most results at home had been excellent. This game was no different. After a slightly shaky start, Town established complete control (another *Festive 50* cracker from Joe Strummer and his gang) with Biggins, King and an own goal putting Salop in an unassailable position, before a late consolation goal for the away team. The return of Graham Turner in midfield made a difference with Rovers unable to counter Town's dominance, despite the presence of 'utility' player Tony Pulis and 'striker' Gary Mabbutt. It looked as though the team from Bristol were in a rut, and needed to get out of it, out of it, out of it, out of it (number 11 in the 1979 *Festive 50* if you're wondering).

Town were ending the year fourth from bottom of the Second Division, zero points above the drop zone but ahead of Rovers and Charlton on goal difference, and Fulham who were bottom. Burnley, one place above us, would be the visitors on New Year's Day. There was uncertainty about what 1980 would bring – would Shrewsbury Town's first season at this level also be their last?

Town Times hadn't printed the league table – perhaps it was too depressing to see the club near the foot of the division all the time? Instead, in the edition for this game, there was a two-page spread of pubs in the locality where you could go and celebrate the new year and toast the club's continued attempts to defy the critics. So Eddie and Margaret encouraged you to have a pint of Wem Best Bitter at The Steam Wagon Inn, Chris and Stan welcomed you to The Old Bush Inn (Bass, chicken in basket, scampi in basket), Arnold and Doreen invited you to The Bricklayer's Arms and Keith and Wendy would be your kind hosts at The Black Horse.

The Lamb Inn at Wrockwardine Wood promised, 'Live Hammond Organ music will be played all over the festive season.' Me, I'd just turned 16, so I was happy with a few swigs of bottled cider and some 'Teenage Kicks'.

* * *

FA Cup Interlude 3

In the previous FA Cup interludes in this book, Shrewsbury's experiences in the first two rounds of the competition during the 1970s were covered. When it comes to the third round, the club's sole victory in that decade at this stage does rather stand out. And the win threw up a plum tie in the next round which signalled a potential path to glory.

6 January 1979
FA Cup third round
Shrewsbury Town 3 Cambridge United 1
Attendance: 7,416

Before this tie, Town had battled through to this stage of the FA Cup on four occasions in the 1970s only to be defeated each time. Losing 2-0 to Derby away in 1972 was nothing to be ashamed of – the Rams won the league that year. There were other away losses to teams from higher levels (QPR in 1977 and Blackburn in '78). The 2-1 home defeat to Fourth Division Bradford in January 1976 was a result that left Town red-faced in embarrassment. In the 1979/80 season described in this book, Shrewsbury's debut in the Second Division meant their first direct entry into round three and a 5-1 clobbering at Millwall. Best not to dwell on that one.

Back in the latter half of 1978, assured away victories against Mansfield and Doncaster in rounds one and two gave the team and fans hope that they could overcome Cambridge United at the next stage, even though the U's played in the Second Division, one level above Shrewsbury at the time. But Town were in fine form and on Boxing Day had earned a valuable point at the Third Division leaders Watford, to remain just behind them in the table. Gaining promotion to the second tier for the first time was surely the priority, but a nice little cup run wouldn't go amiss.

As this period was right in the midst of the so-called 'Winter of Discontent', with widespread public strikes, the football was probably a very welcome distraction. However, in early 1979 the country was also hit by a bout of extremely cold weather with freezing conditions, blizzards and heavy snowfall having a serious impact on the UK, including football fixtures. Due to the icy conditions, Town's previous two games had been postponed so it was some relief that the Gay Meadow pitch was given the go-ahead for this third-round match.

In fact, it was one of only four cup games that took place on 6 January 1979. There was an eventful clash at Hillsborough where, in terrible, snowy conditions, Sheffield Wednesday came from a goal down to draw 1-1 with Arsenal. The equaliser arrived soon after keeper Pat Jennings had been pelted with snowballs by home supporters behind the goal. Amazingly, this tie went to a fourth replay before the Gunners finally scraped their way through, eventually going on to win the trophy that year. There was less drama at St Andrew's as Burnley beat Birmingham 2-0, while at an icy Filbert Street, Leicester City's Keith Weller donned his famous white tights and proceeded to skate through the Norwich City defence to score a cracking individual goal. That was the main game on *Match of the Day* that night, but the cameras were also in Shropshire to film the other playable fixture that day.

My teenage match report at the time stated, 'Maguire scored early and Shrewsbury never looked like losing to Second Division Cambridge. Sammy Chapman scored a great goal.' Graham Turner notched the other one and Town were in the hat. The winter of 1979 had been a difficult time for many, with crippling strikes and Arctic weather, but Shrewsbury's performances were warming the cockles of the fans' hearts and making us smile. And when that wooden ball was plucked out of the velvet bag with Manchester City's number on it – well, scenes! A famous First Division team full of internationals and a man in a fedora hat would soon be heading to Shropshire. Town were second in the league and in the fourth round of the FA Cup for the first time since 1966. Surely things couldn't get any better, could they?

* * *

Home Matchday 12
'Rise'

The 3-1 victory over Bristol Rovers in late December had given the club and fans a much-needed boost and now on the first day of the 1980s, Shrewsbury were aiming to maintain their excellent home form against lowly Burnley to continue ascending the table. Unlike some of the upwardly mobile teams in the Second Division at this time, the Turf Moor club were in steady decline and being so lowly was a new sensation for their supporters. In 1974, Burnley had finished sixth in the First Division and were beaten by Newcastle in the FA Cup semi-final. They then beat Leicester 1-0 in what was the final play-off to establish third place in the competition. Not a lot of people know that.

Their team of that period fielded some quality footballers such as Martin Dobson, Leighton James and Paul Fletcher. The Magpies also beat the Clarets in the Texaco Cup Final that year but more recently Burnley had lifted the Anglo-Scottish Cup in late 1978. At the start of this new decade, long-serving keeper Alan Stevenson was still at the club, Dobson had returned after a period at Everton and forward Billy Hamilton was banging in a few goals and would go on to score a couple in the 1982 World Cup finals. In general though, Burnley were sliding downwards and by May this had culminated in relegation to the Third Division for the first time in their history. It would get worse. The nadir was at the end of the 1986/87 season when a single point separated one of the Football League's founders from an ignominious descent into the Conference.

In his piece for *Town Times*, Graham Turner had said that he was 'confident that despite our present position, we will be playing Second Division football next season'. Over 10,000 flocked to the Meadow on that cold, wintry afternoon, most of them hoping that the boss would be right.

1 January 1980
Shrewsbury Town 2 Burnley 0
Attendance: 10,506

As a new decade beckons it is customary to look back at the previous ten years. In Malcolm Starkey's column in the programme that day, the club secretary (and former Town player) made the sensible decision to focus on the successes of 1979 as it had simply been the best year in the club's history. He started by describing the FA Cup run and the famous victories over Cambridge and Manchester City before recalling the heroic defeat against Wolves in the quarter-final. He mentioned the first promotion to the second tier in the club's history and how beating Wrexham in the Welsh Cup Final had put the cherry on the top of a magnificent season. Graham Turner's guidance as a first-time manager was also acknowledged.

Away from the playing side, Starkey revealed how pleasantly surprised the club had been to have sold over 2,600 season tickets. At £12 for a junior version, I was pretty chuffed too. We'd already beaten Chelsea, Wrexham and West Ham in the inaugural Second Division campaign – decent value for money so far. Starkey also talked about inflation and having to break the club transfer record (£100,000 was paid for John Dungworth). He bemoaned the necessity of having to erect some barriers around the pitch but commended the innovative new 'ansafone system' which could 'take up to 40 simultaneous calls'.

Starkey was also positive about the improvements made to the drainage of the pitch. Playing conditions on the Gay Meadow surface were certainly better than days gone by, but this still did not prevent balls from being hoofed skywards and up over the Riverside stand before plopping down into the River Severn, which ran adjacent to the ground. And that was when Our Man Fred was called into action. As soon as a ball was booted river-wards, Fred Davies would lift his coracle on to his back and scuttle off down the tunnel. He had the unique job of retrieving balls from the Severn on matchdays.

When it had rained heavily and the river was up and flowing more quickly than usual, I did wonder whether the club secretary ever got a late-night phone call along these lines, 'Hello Mr Starkey. It's Fred. I've got the ball, but I'm afraid I'm in Worcester. Any chance of a lift back to Shrewsbury?' One man and his coracle are an integral part of the club's history and Fred's role was (and is) known far beyond the borders of Shropshire. The original vessel used to retrieve balls was put on show at the National Football Museum in Manchester. As well as having autographs of all the Town players of that era, I'm very pleased to say that I also have the signature of Fred the Coracle Man.

In my Burnley match report that day, I noted that it was, 'An exciting game with a brilliant atmosphere. Salop played well.' The first goal, yet again, was from a trademark corner and near-post flick, when not for the first time, the ball was bravely headed in by Jake King. Maguire rifled in the second to send the fans home happy and start the new decade with a victory. For the away fans trudging back to their cars, coaches or the station, little did they know what further grimness, soul-searching and woe was heading their way – in the 18 games remaining, Burnley registered one win, scored a measly 11 times and went down, without even managing to produce a convincing whimper. For the

Town fans it was a different matter; perhaps we could now fully share the manager's optimism that this team was more than capable of performing well at this level and that Town would have at least one more season in the Second Division during the 1980s. As Burnley went into a tailspin, The Shrews were now navigating their way upwards to safety.

Home Matchday 13
'London Calling'

It was January 1980 and the introduction to the visitors in the programme for the game at Cambridge was entitled 'Spotlight on the Champions'. The article demonstrated some kinship and solidarity with their fellow 'small club', as it pointed out that many 'experts' had tipped Shrewsbury to return straight back to the Third Division but those 'experts' may have underestimated Town as they had done with the Abbey Stadium side the previous season. The camaraderie didn't extend to the pitch and it was a comfortable 2-0 win for the U's.

Despite this 12th away defeat, in his regular column for *Town Times* for the next fixture, player-manager Graham Turner remained upbeat. He was fully aware that the main topic of conversation for fans was whether Town could survive their first season in the Second Division.

'Well I believe we can!' he wrote. This was commendably optimistic, but everyone going to this game knew that these rivals south of the border would absolutely love it if they could put a big old spanner in the Shropshire club's home form.

19 January 1980
Shrewsbury Town 1 Cardiff City 2
Attendance: 6,870

In the 1970s, Shrewsbury encountered Cardiff City as many times in the Welsh Cup as they did in the league (three each). The Bluebirds played most of the decade in the Second Division and even when they were relegated in 1974/75, they bounced straight back up the following season. That was the period when I first saw Town play Cardiff. It was a 3-1 victory in front of over 7,000. In my teenage match report at the time, I noted that it was, 'A super game. Salop played well and there was quite a lot of crowd trouble.' There was clearly no love lost between the teams and their respective supporters. And it was the Welsh Cup clashes that largely fuelled the animosity. Town had lost 2-1 in a semi-final in 1974 but gained revenge three years later when they won the two-legged final 4-2 on aggregate. Sadly, the rules forbade winning English teams from entering the European Cup Winners' Cup via the competition, which, to a young fan, seemed very unfair. So, the following season it was Cardiff City, representing Wales, who came up against Austria Wien in the first round. Well, at least they lost.

My initiation to the Welsh Cup had been in 1975 for a fifth-round tie against Bangor City along with 1,038 others. Very little expense had been spent (2p to be precise) on the two-sided printout on yellow paper claiming to be the 'official programme'. In the previous round Llanidloes had been crushed 9-0 so we could probably expect another goal fest against this team from North Wales. The game ended 1-1. 'Didn't we have a loverly time, the day we went to Bangor for the replay?' some fans may have sung, after Town came away 1-0 winners, but I wasn't one of those lucky few who had made that trip. I also saw Shrewsbury botch a semi-final replay on penalties to another great 'Welsh' outfit, Hereford United, in 1976, but a year later I heartily enjoyed a 4-1 walloping of Wrexham at the same stage. Undoubtedly my Welsh Cup highlight was going to both legs of the final in the 'Spirit of 79' season. Even if Wrexham had drafted in John Toshack, John Charles and Ivor Allchurch in their prime, with David Lloyd George as manager, I don't think anything could have stopped Town from inserting the cherry on the top of their other achievements that season.

For those of a ground-hopping persuasion (you know who you are), the Welsh Cup produced its fair share of obscure footballing locations to tick off. In the 1970s alone, Shrewsbury also travelled to play Porthmadog, Courtaulds Greenfield (Who are ya?!), Pwllheli & District and Bridgend Town. Respect, if you went to any of those games. If you went to them all, massive props – you're a hardcore Town obsessive and quite possibly bonkers. There were some unusual home ties too against Welshpool, Rhyl, Ton Pentre and Nantlle Vale (Where are ya?!). Oswestry Town had been the visitors in the cup earlier that January and Salop had not exactly covered themselves in glory by only drawing 2-2. It would be nice to say that they'd played the kids but this probably wasn't an option – Cross and Maguire were the scorers. Winning the replay 6-1 was more acceptable. Ultimately, the Welsh Cup was good for Shrewsbury Town as the club hold the record for an English club winning the Welsh Cup on the most occasions (six). It's a record that won't change anytime soon – English clubs were barred from entering after 1995.

This Second Division game against Cardiff went to plan for the first 78 minutes. Dungworth had ended his goal drought in the ninth minute and for most of the match it looked like two valuable points for Town. But late on, it all went horribly wrong. Buchanan converted a free kick and three minutes from time, former Tranmere striker Ronnie Moore grabbed the winner. In my brief synopsis of the match, I described it as 'a bad lose' (bad English more like). That was putting it mildly. This serious glitch in Town's excellent home form must have felt like a hammer (or maybe a spanner) blow to the manager and his team. And for the Gay Meadow regulars, conceding two late goals and losing to their arch-rivals was really no laughing matter.

Next up was a fixture against Chelsea, now second behind Newcastle, but who had battered the league leaders 4-0 the previous weekend. Yikes! In the Cardiff programme, Turner had expressed confidence in getting something from Stamford Bridge (perhaps he meant buying a commemorative mug or some other merch from their club shop?), but after this dispiriting home defeat against the Welsh team, and on current away form, such optimism surely now seemed misplaced. Yet there were still plenty of Town fans who shared the manager's faith and would have pored over the large map in the programme in preparation for the forthcoming trip to the capital. London calling indeed. In Graham we trust.

* * *

FA Cup Interlude 4

If you were in a Shropshire home or local pub when the 1979 FA Cup fourth round draw was made, you would have heard whooping, cheering, the odd scream and witnessed some manic jumping around. A plum of a tie had just been plucked out of the velvet bag and a legendary football club from the north-west of England, with a magnificent history and recent successes in Europe under their belt, would soon be on their way to Shrewsbury. This team were chock-full of brilliant players and were led by a charismatic coach. The BBC cameras would be in place, and on an icy pitch, with a large and lively Gay Meadow crowd, maybe, just maybe, an upset was on.

27 January 1979
FA Cup fourth round
Shrewsbury Town 2 Manchester City 0
Attendance: 14,215

City had no thoughts about fielding a second-string side – the FA Cup was a prestigious, desirable target. Thcy would put out a team with an impressive pedigree. Goalkeeper Joe Corrigan had represented England, and Willie Donachie and Dave Watson were also international-level defenders. Asa Hartford oozed class in midfield, while Peter Barnes could bamboozle full-backs and skilfully supply crosses from the left wing for frontmen Brian Kidd and Mick Channon to dispatch. These were talented stars with illustrious careers. Even younger players such as Paul Power and Gary Owen already had considerable top-level experience.

Centre-back Paul Futcher had been the club's record transfer in 1978 and another intriguing signing was Kazimierz Deyna. Along with Alberto Tarantini, Ossie Ardiles and Ricky Villa, the gifted Polish midfielder was among a wave of elite international players to come and play in England after the 1978 World Cup. This influx of world-class overseas footballers was an unbelievably exciting development for fans at the time. Deyna and Ardiles even went on to play together in the successful Allied team in *Escape to Victory*! City were now managed by club legend Tony Book, but Malcolm Allison had just returned in a coaching capacity. Although City's current position in the First Division was disappointing, in the previous month they had knocked AC Milan out of the UEFA Cup, 5-2 on aggregate, so for a team brimming with such quality players, this fixture looked like a mismatch. But you know what they say about the FA Cup.

Demand to see the game was massive and the lines of fans had snaked back into the heart of the town. My mum and dad remember the extraordinary experience of joining the queue in Dogpole, near St Mary's Church, and moving slowly down Wyle Cop and over the English Bridge to secure our tickets. When matchday arrived, the wintry weather threatened the tie, but supporters helped to clear the pitch and referee Ray Toseland from Market Harborough gave it the go-ahead. The teams ran out to a vibrant atmosphere. City players were sporting their stylish away kit with the black and red diagonal sash, the home side wearing the classic blue and amber striped shirt (illustrated by a nice graphic in the *Town Times* centre spread). Shrewsbury were fast out of the blocks and scored in the ninth minute when Maguire raced past Futcher, the £350,000 defender, to score in front of the away fans amassed in the Station End. And early in the second half the home fans' dreams edged closer to reality. As Maguire shaped up to swing over a corner, with delirious supporters standing just behind him, *Match of the Day* commentator David Coleman brilliantly described a magical moment in the club's history, 'Well what a revelation Shrewsbury have been. Full of ideas. Full of confidence and a lot of football. Maguire's corner – Chapman! It's there. The stands at Gay Meadow are SHAKING.'

My teenage match report was less poetic but certainly heartfelt, 'My best ever match. Little Shrewsbury beating mighty Manchester City. A lot of people ran on to the pitch … including me.' Those lucky enough to have seen this magnificent performance by Graham Turner's team will remember the jubilant scenes with a backdrop of hundreds of City fans trooping despondently along the railway line towards the station. It was quite a sight.

This was the only time Town had ventured into the fourth round in the 1970s and now we had joined the last 16. After the match, some large metallic badges were produced, listing the cup triumphs so far and proclaiming 'Show the way'. The Shropshire club were certainly going places. Aldershot away as it turned out. We're gonna need a bigger badge – this FA Cup adventure ain't over yet.

* * *

Home Matchday 14
'I'm in the mood for dancing'

The trip to west London the previous weekend had been one to cherish. Manager Graham Turner's pre-match positivity had been spot on – Town did get something from Stamford Bridge. Big time. His Shrewsbury team had only gone and upset the odds by beating high-flying Chelsea 4-2 on their own manor. What a performance, what a result! John Dungworth netted twice, Jack Keay scored a penalty and Ian Atkins, who had just recovered from chickenpox, was immense, capping it all with a fine fourth goal.

Not that I'd been present to witness this stunning achievement. My personal diary records that I was at the Odeon Cinema, Mardol, enjoying a double bill of *Monty Python and the Holy Grail* and *Blazing Saddles.* Comedy central. It wasn't the first time I'd seen these films, so I really hope I didn't annoy my chums (or anyone else close by) with any 'oh, this bit's hilarious' spoilers prior to the limb severing or deadly rabbit moments. And as legally set out in the schoolboy humour charter, we all guffawed at the beans meanz fartz campfire scene. I expect I found out the Chelsea result when I got home later that day before I sat down to watch *Raid on Rommel* (not a funny film) followed by *Match of the Day.*

Doing the double over the Londoners was certainly a highlight of the season so far but it now had to be backed up with a home win.

9 February 1980
Shrewsbury Town 3 Charlton 1
Attendance: 6,988

I was doing my 'mock' GCSE O levels at this time and my diary recorded how I felt after I'd taken each exam: History (okay), Chemistry (all right), Biology (not bad) and Woodwork CSE Practical (oh dear). I was pretty hopeless at working with wood as evidenced by a rectangular piece of discarded chipboard with the words 'Shrewsbury' clumsily gouged out. At this time, although I did enjoy a game of pool at the pub, football generally took precedence, whether playing it, discussing it or arguing about it at school. I watched as much of it as I could on TV (*Match of the Day*, *Sportsnight*, *Star Soccer*) but nothing beat the live match experience and this Saturday was no different. I'd gone on the bus to Shrewsbury with my mate Puck. We'd looked around the shops and now we stood at our regular haunt, on the Riverside terraces, ready for thrills, spills and goals.

Town were finally beginning to climb the table steadily and were now seventh from bottom, while the visitors Charlton lay in the relegation spots, but were only four points worse off. Nothing less than a victory would suffice to maintain the momentum. On paper, the Addicks didn't look particularly threatening, though they had beaten Town earlier in the season. Their line-up didn't include as many well-known names as most other clubs in the division at the time, but they did have two cool-sounding Danes, Johnny Ostergaard and Viggo Jacobsen, to look out for. By far their most famous player was Derek Hales, the hairy hitman (in terms of his prolific scoring rate that is), who went on to become Charlton's all-time leading goalscorer. But the beardy bagger of goals had no joy at Gay Meadow on this occasion and went off injured late in the game.

It wasn't a classic. Biggins headed the home team into an early lead and though the visitors levelled soon after the break, it was Town's trusty dead-ball routines that were the key to securing a vital two points. Paul Maguire was the creator, swinging over two deadly corner kicks for Dungworth and Jake King to convert. King, the Scottish defender, had an impressive goal tally – he scored three in the last two games of the third division championship-winning season – and had already notched four in that season. Not bad for a full-back.

King started as a 15-year-old apprentice at Shrewsbury and had progressed to club skipper. Earlier in the season, he had even featured in *Shoot!* magazine, looking resplendent in a classic town kit (from a previous season) with the unmistakeable Umbro stripes. With his good looks and slightly spiky hair, the Glaswegian could possibly have been mistaken for a Bay City Roller a few years back. Whether King ever wore tartan trousers is not known, but he was certainly a brilliant performer for Shrewsbury. He made over 300 league appearances, mainly in defence, though Turner sometimes utilised King as a midfielder knowing that he would 'never give less than 100 per cent', as the brief profile in *Shoot!*

stated. King was not only a fine player, with a knack for a crucial goal or two, but his outstanding leadership qualities meant that he went on to manage the Town too in the late 1990s. And even though he also played for Wrexham (scoring twice in a famous game in Porto), Cardiff and managed Telford as well, fans didn't hold this against him. Jake King represented Shrewsbury at many different levels and made a huge contribution during his time with Town. He fully deserves his place as a legend in the club's hall of fame.

The summary of the game in my teenage match report was not exactly ebullient but it did imply that Town had achieved their objective and been in control of the outcome, 'A satisfactory win which Salop never looked like losing.' Charlton manager Andy Nelson was slightly more complimentary in his tribute after the match (and published in the Wrexham programme of 1 March), 'If Shrewsbury manage to stay in the Second Division and establish themselves there, they should present all the medals they can find to the manager. If Graham manages that, I for one, will take my hat off to him.' Praise indeed.

So, with successive victories over London clubs, the fans went home happy, wondering if their team could complete a hat-trick of triumphs over sides from the capital by beating Orient at Brisbane Road in the next fixture. On this form, hopes were high that Town could keep moving on up and not just survive, but actually thrive in League Division Two. I went home happy too and watched *Doctor at Sea* and of course, *Match of the Day*. Rock 'n' roll.

Home Matchday 15
'Together we are beautiful'

February 1980 had been a fine month so far. Town were rocking and rolling. Orient were next in line and the opening column in their programme sounded a stark warning, 'The O's had better watch out. This Shrewsbury outfit are no pushover.' Salop were gaining respect all the time and living up to the build-up, won 1-0. After Chelsea and Charlton, this was the third consecutive victory over London teams, and propelled the club up the Second Division to a respectable 15th position. Sitting comfortably eight points above the relegation zone, with only two points for a win, gave Town some breathing space at last. And today's game offered the juicy prospect of another upset involving a very famous football club.

23 February 1980
Shrewsbury Town 3 Newcastle United 1
Attendance: 10,833

In the week, Nick Owen and the ATV team had been to Gay Meadow to interview manager Graham Turner, no doubt capturing the buoyant mood. It's quite likely that the phrase 'punching above their weight' was used. In contrast, Newcastle were a massive club who had slipped down to the second tier of the pyramid. The Magpies were currently in fourth place with high expectations for promotion, so their visit was hotly anticipated. In *Town Times*, freelance journalist Russell Mulford wrote a piece extolling the joys of smaller clubs earning 'a taste of success', citing Ipswich, Southampton and Norwich in the First Division as examples. He also wished that lesser well-known teams such as Shrewsbury, Watford and Swansea were challenging at the top of the Second Division, stating, 'How much more fun to see the more fashionable sides dumped on their backsides by emerging minnows.' Well, the Salopian reporter must have loved watching Town do the business in this game and he must have also enjoyed subsequent seasons, when the other two clubs he mentioned fulfilled his wishes, achieving considerable success at the top level.

It wasn't only Town hitting peak form in this period that was pressing my buttons, as something else was titillating my fancy: music. On Radio 1 it was David 'Kid' Jensen broadcasting in the late afternoon, a DJ who, in my mind at least, clearly had good taste in music (unlike some of his colleagues who were on earlier in the day). I'd often tape the first 90 minutes of the *John Peel Show* at 10pm (45 minutes on each side of a C90 cassette) hoping to catch something tasty in the net before I dropped off. On telly, Thursday evenings meant *Top of the Pops* and I noted down the standout performances in my diary each week (10 Jan: Skids; 24 Jan: Specials; 7 Feb: Tourists, Chords, Selector). Annie Nightingale, presenting *The Old Grey Whistle Test*, was cool too and appearances by the kind of bands I liked were becoming more frequent on this show.

Punk hadn't really hit our part of rural South Shropshire in a big way, but I had discovered that the Sex Pistols, The Clash, Buzzcocks, Siouxsie and the Banshees and The Stranglers were making exciting, refreshing records with attitude. On trips to Shrewsbury or Wolverhampton I was intrigued by the haircuts, clothes and the paraphernalia adorned by the youths hanging about in the town centres – whether they were proper, plastic or part-time punks didn't really matter. I had also developed an affinity for the sounds and vision that were emerging from the original punk scene. During this period, I started to plot a graph of 'New Wave songs in the Top 75'. The trend peaked in September 1979 with 28 entries then tailed off but by the end of the year I'd given up logging these findings (and run out of space).

Now I was more interested in getting closer to the action. In January 1980, the first UK Indie Singles Chart was compiled and published. I rushed out and bought the first number one: Spizz Energi's effervescent 'Where's Captain Kirk?' On the evening of the day Town had defeated Orient, a group of us watched local group Blind Eye play the Village Hall in Newcastle. Essentially, they were a rock covers band, but we were more energised by their version of 'Pretty Vacant' than anything they did by Free or Status Quo. On the Wednesday before the Newcastle game, I experienced my first 'real' gig (I'm not counting Steeleye Span as my folks took us to that one) at The Music Hall, Shrewsbury. Support act Wreckless Eric performed a brilliant, lively set which pretty much blew the headliners, Squeeze, off the stage. In fact, messrs Tilbrook, Difford and keyboard player Jools Holland had nearly walked away anyway after a small coterie of mindless punks started flobbing in their direction. I recall the drummer getting understandably miffed when globules of spit landed on him and for a few moments it looked as though this unseemly incident was going to end in some argy-bargy. Slightly ironic, as *ArgyBargy* was the title of Squeeze's latest album, the one they were trying to plug. Musically, things had been livening up nicely, but it wasn't going to take the edge off my appetite for the big game.

Gay Meadow wasn't at capacity for the Newcastle game, but the Toon Army had filled the Station End. The Magpies' strong attacking line-up that day featured Billy Rafferty, local lad Alan Shoulder, who went on to score 21 goals in this campaign, and Peter Withe. Withe had been in the Nottingham Forest team that won the First Division in 1977/78 and went on to score Aston Villa's winning goal in the European Cup Final against Bayern Munich in 1982. On the cover and back page of the programme for this match were two unsung members of the Town side, players who would not reach the lofty heights that Withe did, but nevertheless were mainstays of this successful period in Shrewsbury's history. On the back page was Oswestry-born full-back Carleton Leonard, who had been man of the match against Orient and was a reliable, two-footed defender who played most of the season, apart from a short period out with injury. Leonard's 298 appearances for Town is a very respectable total. It was usually Tony Larkin who stepped in to deputise at the back, proving that he was another crucial member of the squad who could be depended on to do a solid job. Steve Cross, shown doing a characteristic shimmy in the photo on the *Town Times* cover, didn't appear in this game but did a stalwart job in midfield over the years, making over 250 appearances and scoring 33 goals. He was inducted in the club's hall of fame in 2013. Both Leonard and Cross had also played vital parts in the previous season's championship win so as far as I was concerned, they were already assured of fame and legendary status.

In the match, the minnows from Shropshire dumped the Geordie giants on their backsides. Maguire, King, and Biggins were Town's scorers, with Shoulder converting a late consolation penalty. The Meadow was rocking. On the pitch, February 1980 had been perfect for Town, and Turner would soon be receiving the Bell's Manager of the Month award. Spizz Energi were still topping the alternative charts at the end of February and Blondie's 'Atomic' had replaced Kenny Rogers at number one. It all sounded good to me.

Home Matchday 16
'And the beat goes on'

Relegation? You're 'avin' a laugh. Town were on a storming run of five consecutive victories including a 1-0 away win at local rivals Wrexham the previous Saturday. I didn't go to the Racecourse Ground on that occasion, but I had enjoyed some good times at the ground in the past. I'd got my first Town away day under the belt in January 1978, as diarised, 'Went on train. 0-0 (good).' Later on, in the evening, I went to a talk by the explorer Colonel Blashford-Snell at Bishop's Castle Legion Hall. What a day! A few years earlier I'd been on a school trip to watch Wales play Austria in the European Championship in front of 30,000 noisy Welsh supporters, when current Wrexham manager Arfon Griffiths netted the only goal. Oh what a night, mid-November, 1975. The only downside was on the coach journey there, after school-mate Phil Davies consumed a few too many pineapple chunks, those yellow, hard-boiled, sugary sweets, which resulted in some very visible unpleasantness in the aisle next to the back seats. I'd been to the match celebrating the centenary of the Welsh FA in 1976 when England won 2-1. Peter Taylor, then playing for Crystal Palace in the Third Division, came on as substitute and scored the winner on his debut. Ray Kennedy had got the first and Swansea's Alan Curtis knocked in a late consolation goal. I also saw Scotland draw 0-0 in the (much missed) home internationals in 1977 when Denis Law was mobbed by the Tartan Army outside the ground. 'Denis, will ya ha my baby?' one large, kilted Scotsman bellowed, to roars of laughter.

The best match I'd watched at the Racecourse was the FA Cup quarter-final between Wrexham and Arsenal in 1978 when the Gunners won 3-2 en route to the final.

My most recent visit had been the previous May when Steve Biggins had scored in the first leg of the Welsh Cup Final. Yes, I had fond memories of the Racecourse, and though pleased that Salop had won again to maintain this excellent form, I wished I'd been standing on those familiar terraces to witness it.

After a shaky start to the season, the team had now reached the heady heights of mid-table in the Second Division. Next up were a side just behind table-toppers Chelsea, the second-best football club in the Second Division from England's second city: the Blues of Birmingham would be making the short journey to the Meadow.

8 March 1980
Shrewsbury Town 1 Birmingham City 0
Attendance: 14,801

On this day, my pre-match routine was summarised in a brief diary entry, 'Went on bus to Salop, mucked around shops, had chips.' Let me expand: the shops I probably visited (or 'mucked around') were as follows: for general browsing, John Menzies; for sports equipment browsing, Alltrees or Salopian Sports ('Dave Pountney, the owner, played for Town, you know'). Just before Christmas one year I spotted my dad walking away from Alltrees carrying a long, rectangular cardboard box. I wondered if it was football nets for the garden. I felt guilty having inadvertently ruined the surprise factor, but I didn't let on. On the big day, I feigned surprise but didn't have to feign the delight. For 7in single browsing and the odd purchase it was Charlie's Records or Durrants – I didn't buy albums at this time: 1) they were too dear 2) I could borrow LPs from friends and tape them.

I had just turned 16 so pubs in town weren't a viable option quite yet. We sometimes hooked up with mates from Church Stretton in the main town square. On one such occasion, at this very location, I remember asking one of them if the badge pinned on his donkey jacket was Shakespeare. It was Lenin. Ouch. But a mistake that any teen with extremely limited political awareness (and less than perfect eyesight) could have made. Anyway, I liked to think I was a student of a more literary bent, as evidenced by my extensive reading of the works of Jack Higgins, James Herbert and Sven Hassel. Indeed, I was hoping to study English Literature at A level and felt confident that all would be fine, as long as those authors were on the syllabus.

Back to the pre-match build-up in town: if we'd caught the earlier bus and had more time, after a decent mucking around session, we'd amble down Wyle Cop, then swing right at the bottom, and stroll along St Julian's Friars to cross Greyfriars Bridge. Built in 1880, and not Shropshire's most famous iron bridge, this construction is small but perfectly formed. Not that late-19th-century feats of engineering were on our minds. Nope – we were heading towards Jack's Fish Saloon and most likely wondering whether to have a chicken and mushroom pie, a spam fritter or a battered saveloy with our chips. Tough call, but one that was usually resolved without too much fuss.

Refreshed, we'd continue along Longden Coleham, meeting the early match day crowds at the junction with the English Bridge, before turning left on the approach road (the 'Narrows') to Gay Meadow. I'd buy a *Town Times* programme and usually be in position on the Riverside by 2pm. Unlike some, I didn't think this was ridiculously early, as it gave me ample time to scrutinise the programme (I'd moved on from making any changes to the line-ups on the back cover – hah, that was for kids or nerds!), enjoy some pre-match banter and soak up the atmosphere.

I don't recall encountering any Blues fans in the town that day – perhaps they just weren't as interested in the latest new wave singles on coloured vinyl or post-punk records in picture sleeves as I was – but the Brummie hordes were certainly out in force at the ground. It was the largest home attendance of the season and my teenage match report mentioned the 'incredible atmosphere', but also that 'there was nearly a riot'. Twice the game was stopped as Birmingham fans spilled on to the pitch from the overcrowded Station End. These incidents were a serious concern and kept police and Red Cross teams very busy that day.

The visitors had some notable names in their side. Colin Todd was an accomplished defender with poise and numerous England caps, while Mark Dennis had a rather different reputation as a tough-tackling left-back who got sent off 12 times in his career. In midfield, Blues had ex-Hammer Alan Curbishley alongside Scottish international Archie Gemmill, who was renowned for his tenacity and skill. Not only had Gemmill won three First Division championship medals and a European Cup from his time at Derby County and Nottingham Forest, but he'd also scored *that* amazing individual goal against Holland in the 1978 World Cup finals, his mazy dribble later immortalised in the film *Trainspotting*. In attack, Keith Bertschin ended up with 18 goals for the campaign. Frank Worthington was only used as a late substitute and didn't get time to work his magic. This was a quality team who would go on to achieve promotion that season.

On the day, though, Birmingham just weren't good enough to come away with anything from Shrewsbury. It was another outstanding result for the home team with brilliant performances from David Tong, who outshone the opposition midfield and earned my man-of-the-match award (8/10), Paul Maguire, who fired in the winner just before half-time, and Colin Griffin, superb in defence. Griffin, the moustachioed centre-half, took his role very seriously and his stern, no-nonsense demeanour on the pitch and robust challenges conveyed the impression that he was well hard. The Town faithful were very thankful to have his solid, dependable presence in the back four. The sort of chap you'd be relieved and grateful to have in your gang, rather than any other gang. After 400 appearances for the club, it's no wonder that Griffin was inducted as a Town hall of fame legend. Shrewsbury had now won six games on the bounce in the Second Division. Such fun!

Home Matchday 17
'Dance yourself dizzy'

I have a confession to make. I was once a Shropshire White. Yep, 'fraid so. Full disclosure: Town weren't my only love, nor even my first love – I was also infatuated with Leeds United. And one of my idols, whose pictures were blu-tacked to my bedroom walls, would be playing for the visitors in the next home game in late March. However, my relationship with Leeds was mostly long-distance – visits to Elland Road or to Midlands grounds such as Molineux to watch the Whites had been rare. Watching Town was far more accessible and let's face it, pleasurable, at this time. I was attending every Shrewsbury home game courtesy of my £12 junior season ticket and as we were on such a roll, my local team were now the main object of my affection.

Even though the six-match winning run had come to an abrupt end at Leicester, Salop had bounced back by beating Watford 1-0 at Vicarage Road with Dungworth getting the winner, again going some way to justifying his price tag. At this point, Town got a two-page feature in *Match* entitled 'Turner puts the Gay back in Meadow'. The piece recounted the 'Shrewsbury Revival' since the first day of the year and cited Stamford Bridge as a turning point in fortunes. The manager talked about the team never losing their 'self belief' and his satisfaction at looking at the league table now, but he also warned against complacency and the importance of keeping 'up the tempo'. QPR were next in the firing line.

29 March 1980
Shrewsbury Town 3 Queens Park Rangers 0
Attendance: 9,050

My passion for Leeds had begun in the early 1970s when they were one of the best teams in Europe. Their popularity in the world of football was perhaps not quite at the same high level but this didn't deter me from acquiring a cache of badges, diaries, scarves, mugs, a pennant, autograph books, and a coat hook. I even had a tie. When my Shrewsbury-born dad got a job back in Shropshire and we moved to the Bishop's Castle area, I soon found out that it was considered acceptable to support both a top tier team *and* Town. In my group of mates, there were fans of Spurs (Griff), Liverpool (Ged), West Ham (Penguin) and Ipswich (Puck). In Clun, a small settlement a few miles away from my home, most of the locals supported Chelsea for some reason. But then again, most of these lads also had Status Quo and Kiss badges sewn on their denim jackets too and did 'the Ace' at local dances. There's no accounting for poor taste.

But at the time LUFC had the biggest contingent of followers (me, my brother Steven, Boris, Nige, Derv and Fred) and we enjoyed occasional trips to Elland Road and away games organised by the Shropshire Whites, the Salopian branch of Leeds United supporters. It was just a shame that Leeds really weren't much cop at this time. Kevin Hird was not a Billy Bremner, Jeff Chandler no 'Sniffer' Clarke. A little harsh, a lot true. In this period, Town were getting far more of my love and attention.

It was Tony Currie, the former Sheffield United and Leeds star, who was one of my all-time favourite players, an honour shared with luminaries such as Peter Lorimer,

Mario Kempes and Paul Maguire. The gifted midfield maestro was now playing a key role in QPR's push for promotion, directing play at the heart of their formation. I'd seen Currie score for Leeds against Wolves and also witnessed his cracker in an England friendly against Hungary on a school trip to Wembley in 1978 – boy, the Shropshire Whites posse went mad at that moment, I can tell you!

Although this was a good QPR side, managed by Tommy Docherty and featuring future England goalkeeper Chris Woods and stylish defender Glenn Roeder, it wasn't a patch on the 1975/76 vintage. This was the team who had produced a superb 2-0 victory over Liverpool on the opening day of that season before the *Match of the* Day cameras. The game is remembered for a brilliant flowing move finished off by Gerry Francis, which later won the goal of the season award. Soon after that match, Town were drawn at home to QPR in the League Cup second round. How exciting was that for young (and older) Salop fans? The team from Loftus Road were on fire! Francis was England captain! It was the first 'big' club I'd seen at Gay Meadow and their second-half performance that night was mesmerising, resulting in a comprehensive 4-1 outcome. Town had been outclassed by one of the best teams to play at our ground that decade. QPR went on to finish second, their highest ever position, a point behind champions Liverpool.

In March 1980, though, the west London outfit were well below par on their visit to Shrewsbury. Luckily for Town, deadly frontman Clive Allen didn't play. Jack Keay was first on the scoresheet with a penalty and player-manager Graham Turner headed a fine second. After defender Bob Hazell had been sent off, there was no way back for Rangers and Steve Biggins crowned another impressive display from the home side with the third goal. Currie had shown his class with some long-range shots, but goalkeeper Bob Wardle excelled to maintain a clean sheet. After the game, Turner acknowledged that Town's Second Division status was virtually assured now. Perhaps my mood was slightly dampened when I heard that Leeds had lost at West Brom that day, but probably only fleetingly. My true love was kitted out in blue and amber. I only had eyes for Town.

* * *

FA Cup Interlude 5

For whatever reason, sometimes you miss a key game and it turns out to be a classic. I'm not totally sure why I wasn't at the Recreation Ground for the original FA Cup fifth round tie against Fourth Division Aldershot in February 1979. Maybe inclement weather? Maybe my parents didn't want me to go on a school night? Anyway, future Shrewsbury striker John Dungworth put the Shots ahead twice, only for Maguire to reply first before Tong lobbed their keeper at the death to force a replay.

I do know why I wasn't at the return game at the Meadow though, which Town won 3-1 (after extra time), with two from Biggins and a rare Carleton Leonard scorcher. I had signed up for a school minibus trip to The Hawthorns to watch a fourth-round clash between West Brom and Leeds that had already been postponed on multiple occasions. Thus, just as Salop were heading to the quarter-final, I was cheering on Leeds as they recovered from being 3-1 down to snatch a late equaliser. In the minibus after the game, as we breathlessly took in what we'd just seen, a fellow schoolboy passenger remarked earnestly that the game 'had been a credit to British football'. The comment was met with sniggers and scoffing from the rest of us. Town would now play Wolves in the quarters. Leeds, after their heroic comeback, lost 2-0 in the replay and were out. At least there wouldn't be any further conflicts of interest.

Here's what happened next, as recounted in my unexpurgated match reports of the time, with sincere apologies to Hugh McIlvanney, Brian Glanville, David Lacey, Henry Winter et al.

10 March 1979
FA Cup sixth round
Wolverhampton Wanderers 1
Shrewsbury Town 1
Attendance: 40,946

'An all-ticket match with a great atmosphere, Shrewsbury took 10,000 fans. In the first half it was pretty equal but Wolves missed quite a few chances. In the second half there was a lot of Wolves pressure but Town's defence was great especially Bob Wardle who was magnificent. Finally the pressure paid off when Bill Rafferty scored a good goal. Surely it was all over, Shrewsbury fans kept on singing though and with two minutes left Maguire ran into the penalty area and was brought down by Daniel. Penalty! We all went wild. Ian Atkins scored it and soon after the whistle went. Shrewsbury had miraculously done it again, now could they do the job at the Gay Meadow. It was a good match and was shown on *Star Soccer*.'

13 March 1979
FA Cup sixth round replay
Shrewsbury Town 1 Wolverhampton Wanderers 3
Attendance: 16,279

'Another all-ticket match. It was a capacity crowd and Wolves brought a lot of supporters. Wolves scored first through Willie Carr. That was the score at half-time. Shrewsbury weren't finding their rhythm and Wolves were. Then Steve Daley crossed from the left and Billy Rafferty headed a great goal. Then Richards was brought down and it was a penalty. Peter Daniel settled the match when he drove the ball hard and low past Wardle. Shrewsbury got a consolation goal near the end through Jack Keay. It was the biggest crowd I had seen at Shrewsbury.'

Thinking about it, perhaps the style and quality of my writing hasn't developed that much over the years!

It had been a great cup run, the furthest the club had ever been in the competition, and now Town could focus on going up to the Second Division, which would be another, arguably even more impressive, historic milestone.

* * *

Home Matchday 18
'Rough Boys'

I'm hoping that you've been paying attention and have gathered by now that Shrewsbury not only got promoted by winning the Third Division championship, but had also pushed on with a remarkable run of results in their inaugural second tier campaign and were very close to guaranteeing at least one more season at this level. Good effort chaps! Fresh from a comfortable 3-0 victory over QPR three days previously, there was no reason to doubt that Town's fine home form would not continue against mid-table Preston, particularly when Biggins opened the scoring after only ten minutes. Unfortunately, things didn't go quite to plan in this game and a member of England's 1966 World Cup-winning team would be leaving Shrewsbury that night with a smile on his face, albeit not the toothless grin that he was famous for.

1 April 1980
Shrewsbury Town 1 Preston North End 3
Attendance: 8,643

After an illustrious playing career, Nobby Stiles, the former Manchester United midfielder, had hung up his boots and taken over the managerial reins at Preston in 1977, winning promotion in his first full season. This wasn't the first time that England players from that famous 1966 team had appeared in Shropshire in recent times. At the Meadow earlier in the season, Geoff Hurst had experienced a very bad day at the office as Chelsea's boss. Bobby Charlton had worn the blue and amber of Town, faring better in a friendly against Zambia in 1978 and most of the players from that triumphant England line-up had even appeared at the Bucks Head in 1976, as part of Telford United's centenary celebrations. In the friendly that evening, the veteran internationals ran out 4-0 winners and in my personal match report I noted, 'Old England played well and showed up Telford, which doesn't take much!' After the game, in the scramble to bag the autographs of true legends, the car Bobby Moore was sitting in the back of, slowly reversed over my foot. A few seconds earlier I had managed to get the World Cup-winning former England captain's signature so the slight shock of that manoeuvre and some bruised toes seemed a price worth paying.

Back in 1980, Preston hadn't lost in four away games so were full of confidence. Their two most well-known players were in defence. Francis Burns had been in the same United squad as Stiles when they won the European Cup in 1968, while ex-Magpie John Blackley had represented Scotland. With Town's good home form set against the visitors' excellent away record, a draw looked the most likely outcome. I was confident though and had also planned to travel up to Burnley on Easter Saturday, a few days later. This wouldn't be my first away game that season – I had been to Filbert Street two weeks earlier. What excitement to follow Town away, to sing your heart out for the lads, to punch the air as the teams run out, to go ape at an away goal. At that match,

Leicester scored in the first minute and all the fervour was extinguished in a moment. Bugger. The high-flying Foxes went on to win 2-0 and Town's six-game winning run was over. Nothing special on the pitch, nothing memorable off it either.

It wasn't always that way with away days though. In Shrewsbury's 1978/79 championship-winning season, my mate Griff and I decided to go to Tranmere Rovers on a Monday in October. We were 14 and it was a school night – what on earth were we thinking?! As we legged it away from a pack of feral scallies from Birkenhead who were chasing us around the unsegregated section of Prenton Park and onto the pitch (as the game continued), the decision to attend this one was beginning to seem a tad unwise. The adrenalin was certainly pumping as we made our escape, but the experience wasn't exactly fun. When Town went 2-0 down, it looked like it was going to be a thoroughly miserable night on the Wirral. Then up stepped Ian Atkins to save the evening with two goals to nick a draw. The Salopian fans were in fine voice as the coach headed away from the ground until a brick crashed through a window a couple of seats behind us. Luckily no one was hurt but it was a chilly coach ride back to Shropshire that night. We'd survived to recount the Tales of Tranmere Away with pride at school the next day.

The Preston game was an entertaining contest in front of a decent crowd but a Keay own goal and two strikes from Steve Elliot sealed victory for the visitors. This wasn't a joyful night for Town but Nobby would be sporting a big grin, with or without his teeth in. We were hoping that in the next fixture, we'd get to watch a thriller up at Burnley and come back with two points on the road. It was 0-0. The Claret programme had a prominent advert for Champagne Saturday at Angels, 'Burnley's No 1 nitespot', but I doubt the locals were in the mood for celebrating much as the Turf Moor side were on a terrible run of form and heading inexorably towards relegation. Town avoiding the drop would unquestionably merit some cork-popping down at Tiffany's nightclub, Shrewsbury.

Home Matchday 19
'Another nail in my heart'

After some brilliant victories in March, Town's results had taken a dip with a home defeat by Preston and that draw at off-form Burnley. Given the fact that the club had been over-achieving in the previous month, this was understandable and forgivable. The most important thing was that Shrewsbury had secured safety from relegation and would be playing at this level again next season. In his regular column in *Town Times*, Graham

Turner acknowledged this fact, but also confirmed, 'Our target is now to finish inside the top half of the Second Division.' The next opponents were Sunderland and their primary objective was promotion to the First Division. Again, a serious test lay ahead.

8 April 1980
Shrewsbury Town 1 Sunderland 2
Attendance: 12,346

This was the third season that the club had gone with the newspaper-sized and styled matchday programme. For every home game, 20p would get you 12 pages with a Town player photographed in action on the cover, superimposed on a light blue background (Acker was making his second appearance of the season for this one). The all-important match ball donor was highlighted on the front too (Octopus Electrical Ltd for this edition, if you're curious). In terms of other content, 'Pro File' candidates seemed to have run out (well, it was a small squad I suppose) but for this game, there was an interesting article on Jock Fulton. The Scottish scout had discovered many Town players from north of the border over the years: Sammy Irvine and Alex McGregor, plus current stars Keay, King and Maguire. Nice work, Jock.

Match reports, which in the early part of the season had often made quite depressing reading, had been replaced by shots of recent action. A two-page centre spread provided details of the visiting squad including a team group. Helpful guidance was offered on how to get to the next away destination as well as a map, so 'Follow the Town to Luton' advised drivers to take the A5, M6, then at intersection 11 on the M1, then 'follow Dunstable Road and the Football Club is on the right'. Simples. Travel by coach cost £3.50. Another regular feature listed scores and scorers from a previous season (1963/64 this time) plus a few comments, but it couldn't be described as in-depth analysis. Adverts, of course, covered a substantial proportion of the programme and apart from car services, televisions, double glazing and plumbers, there was also information on horse riding, hiring a mobile discotheque or joining the army.

Town Times also contained some insightful pieces written by secretary Malcolm Starkey and editor Bryan Pitchford, but it was the column entitled 'Graham' that fans looked forward to reading most and which now merited and covered a whole page. For this game, Turner had started by praising the Gay Meadow support for their patience and loyalty, particularly in the more difficult earlier, stickier parts of the season. He confirmed that the club were on course to meet the average gate target of 8,500–9,000 per home game.

The visit of Sunderland and their voluminous, fanatical away support was bound to bump up the attendance for this fixture.

The Roker Park side had narrowly missed out on promotion the previous season and were determined not to suffer the same fate again. They were on a great run, undefeated since February, with recent victories over Newcastle and Wrexham in the Easter period. Managed by Ken Knighton, Sunderland had two players with considerable top-level experience: former Leicester City and England full-back Steve Whitworth, and prolific, evergreen striker Bryan 'Pop' Robson. Even though Robson did what he did, grabbing the first goal early on, it was two of the visitors' lesser known players who made the biggest impression on this occasion, at different ends of the pitch. In my teenage match report, I noted, 'Chris Turner, the Sunderland keeper, had a fantastic game.' He stopped virtually everything apart from Trevor Birch's headed equaliser. Offensively, it was Stan Cummins, the diminutive former Middlesbrough forward, who made his mark on the game by scoring the winner; 'a marvellous goal' in my account. But Turner's heroics stood out – I still remember standing in the Wakeman End watching the keeper tip an Atkins rocket over the bar. An astounding save to crown a memorable individual performance.

Town also had a decent goalkeeper in Bob Wardle, who had taken over from Ken Mulhearn at the turn of the year and would retain the green jersey not just for the remainder of this season but as an ever-present for the following two campaigns. In 2016 Wardle was voted by fans into a Shrewsbury Town all-time XI on the club website. The team had a good defensive unit at this time but if the back four was breached, you felt confidence in the keeper. He was one of my favourite players and my mum, now in her late 80s, still recalls the chant of 'There's only one Bobby Wardle' echoing around Gay Meadow. Wardle's strong performances eventually earned him a transfer to Liverpool, in an exchange deal that saw Steve Ogrizovic heading for Shrewsbury. Unfortunately for Wardle, he didn't ever play for the first team. The Reds' senior custodian, Bruce Grobbelaar, stood in his way between the sticks.

It was another crucial victory for Sunderland and they would remain undefeated until the end of the season, which guaranteed promotion in second place. As a Shrewsbury fan, it had been an exciting game with a good crowd, but Town had lost to a better team. While most supporters were prepared to accept this, Turner was no doubt more disappointed, and with only four league games to go in the club's first season in the Second Division was still reminding the players (and

Original match programme of first Shrewsbury Town game attended v Chesterfield. Lost 1-0 (1 December 1973)

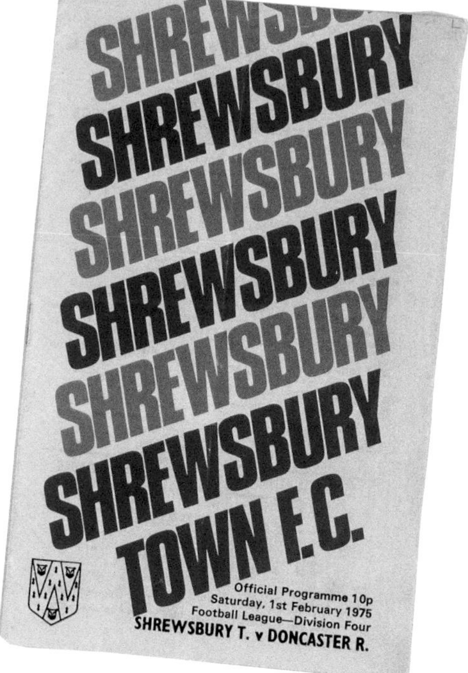

Original match programme for Shrewsbury Town 7 Doncaster Rovers 4 (1 February 1975)

F.A. Cup Fourth Round Special

The official newspaper/programme of Shrewsbury Town Football Club.

January 27th, 1979. Volume 2 Number 16. 20p.

How they reached Round Four

SHREWSBURY TOWN

ROUND ONE —	Mansfield Town Griffin, Atkins	(Away) 2-0
ROUND TWO —	Doncaster Rovers Chapman, Maguire (2)	(Away) 3-0
ROUND THREE —	Cambridge United Turner, Chapman, Maguire	(Home) 3-1

MANCHESTER CITY

ROUND THREE —	Rotherham United	(Home) 0-0 (Away) 4-2 Owen, Barns, Kidd (2)

SHREWSBURY TOWN CLUB FLOREAT SALOPIA FOOTBALL

Shrewsbury Town versus Manchester City

Items from FA Cup run 1978/79: Original match programme for Shrewsbury 2 Man City 0 (27 January 1979) plus centrefold image of team line-ups, sticker and badge.

Football League Division Three

Shrewsbury Town versus Exeter City

Town Times

The official newspaper/programme of Shrewsbury Town Football Club.

May 17th 1979. Volume 2 Number 28 15p

Player of the Year —Jack Keay

Glasgow born Jack Keay was this week named Shrewsbury Town's 'Player of the Year at the annual buffet dance organised by the Football Supporters' Club.

Jack, who topped the poll well ahead of his nearest rivals Jake King and Bob Wardle, joined Shrewsbury at the start of last season after being released by Glasgow Celtic and made twenty first team appearances.

Out of the side at the start of this campaign, he grabbed the chance to establish himself as a regular first team man when Steve Hayes was suspended in early December, and has gone from strength to strength with every game since.

Division 3

	P	W	L	F	A	P
Watford	46	24	10	83	52	60
Swansea	46	24	10	83	61	60
Town	45	20	6	57	40	59
Swindon	46	25	14	74	52	57
Gillingham	45	20	8	63	42	57
Exeter	45	17	13	60	52	49
Colchester	45	16	12	55	54	49
Hull	43	18	14	63	52	47
Chester	46	15	16	62	62	46
Brentford	45	18	18	50	47	45
Southend	46	15	16	51	49	45
Oxford	45	14	14	43	49	45
Plymouth	46	15	17	67	68	44
Blackpool	44	17	18	56	55	43
Sheff Wed	43	11	13	47	49	41
Bury	44	10	14	56	62	40
Rotherham	43	15	18	43	51	40
Chesterfld	43	13	16	49	59	40
Mansfield	42	10	14	46	49	38
Peterboro	44	10	20	41	62	34
Walsall	45	10	23	55	67	32
Tranmere	46	6	24	45	78	28
Lincoln	45	7	27	41	86	25

Jack Keay

Signed by Jake King, the original match programme of Third Division title-clinching game: Shrewsbury 4 Exeter 1 (17 May 1979)

STFC memorabilia from this period:
Matchworn, autographed flag.

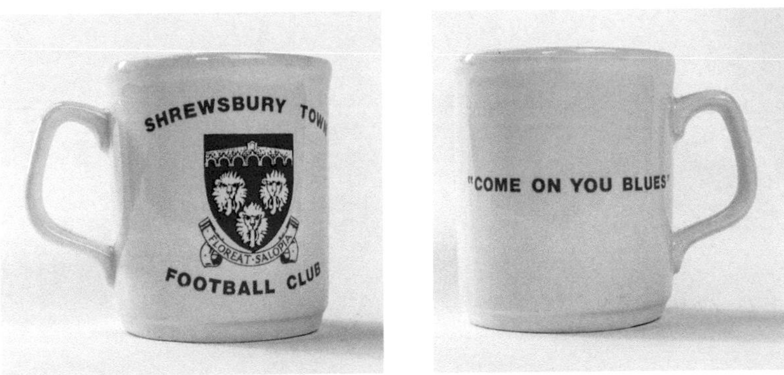

Mug with great name for book about Shrewsbury Town on rear

Door sign from earlier in the 1970s. Not a design classic

And inspired by the period: Paul Maguire T-shirt

KING JAKE!

Skipper's double makes Shrewsbury champions

SHREWSBURY REAC[...] their history in maje[...] champions of the third [...] And just to make it [...] Jake King set up their [...]

Graham Turner

Team	P	W	D	L	F	A	P
Shrewsbury TOWN	46	21	19	6	61	41	61
Watford	46	24	12	10	83	52	60
Swansea	46	24	12	10	83	71	60
Swindon	46	25	7	14	74	52	57
Gillingham	45	20	17	8	63	42	57

[...] top of the [...] player-manager Graham Turner put his country [...] club's achievement into realistic perspective when he said:

"I'm not promising any wild spending spree, but we can do with a couple of players to strengthen our staff."

Insisted

Champions!

Town sweep into Second Division

It was glory, glory day for Shrewsbury Town after their victory over Exeter City at the Gay Meadow last night.

It meant not only promotion to the Second Division for the first time in their 29 seasons in the League, but going up as champions above Watford and Swansea. And this was their first championship title. For the first time since they entered the League Shrewsbury had [...]

[...] acknowledge the appearances at the front of the directors' box of the players, the rest of the first team squad, and perhaps more than any other individual, the club's young and successful player-manager Graham Turner.

The match opened dramatically with just the start Shrewsbury needed. In the second minute [...]

CHAMPION!

Shrewsbury hit top in style

By KEITH MEADOWS

Shrewsbury 4
Exeter 1

GAY MEADOW gleefully hailed little Shrewsbury as champions of the Third Division last night.

Full-back Jake King popped up as the hero of their finest-ever hour with two neat headers in the first eight minutes.

Ensure

SUPER TOWN

A ticker-tape welcome for Shrewsbury from the fans last night.

Champions! — Graham Turner [...]

Pictures: Bob Croig, Malcolm Mackay.

Cup of success

The moment that makes a long, hard season worthwhile ... Shrewsbury player-manager Graham Turner and skipper Jake King proudly hold aloft the Third Division championship cup they received before last night's Welsh Cup final against Wrexham at the Gay Meadow. See also Page 49.

Turner's tigers do it in style

The whole of Shropshire was still buzzing today with the excitement of Shrewsbury Town's promotion to Division Two for the first time. Congratulations were pouring into the Gay Meadow and player manager Graham Turner paused from opening telegrams to declare: "It was a superb night." Less than 12 hours before, his players had beaten Exeter City 4-1 to clinch the Third Division title.

It was a success which sparked emotional scenes the like of which have never before been seen at the Gay Meadow.

Thousands of fans swarmed over the walls on to the pitch singing, chanting and waving banners.

They refused to budge until Turner and his men had made several appearances in the director's box.

Afterwards, the champagne corks popped in [...]

By Bob Davies

[...] and the club on their success.

There was civic praise, too, for Shrewsbury.

Councillor Bernard Lingen, today elected Mayor of Shrewsbury and Atcham, referred to their achievements in his Mayor-making speech and promised the club a civic reception as soon as possible.

[...] police officers who worked long hours yesterday to deal with the extra traffic in town for both the West Mid show and the football match.

As some of the excitement of last night died down, Turner was able to take stock. He declared: "Looking at it realistically, it was a tremendous night [...]"

Jake's double bonus

Shrewsbury Town skipper Jake King can look forward to a £200 bonus after the victory over Exeter.

Sports shop owner Peter Alltree offered the pay out as an incentive to any Shrewsbury player who scored twice in the crucial game. And King duly obliged with a brace inside the first eight minutes.

All lit up with somewhere to go ... Division Two. Non-smoker Graham Turner, the king of [...] Meadow, celebrates with a cigar last [...]

Selection of newspaper headlines/cuttings after winning Division Three championship (May 1979)

SHREWSBURY IN DIVISION TWO FOR FIRST TIME

UP UP AND AWAY

PROMOTION

Back: Steve Hayes, Bob Wardle, Ken Mulhearn, Steve Cross; middle: John Malam, Tony Larkin, Dave Tong, Carlton Leonard, Ian Atkins, Jack Keay, Trevor Birch, Graham Turner; front: D

Ken Mulhearn · Jake King · Colin Griffin · Jackie Keay · Tony Larkin · David Tong · Ian Atkins · Jimmy Lindsay · Stephen Cross · Steve Biggins · Paul Maguire · Trevor Birch

WE ARE THE CHAMPIONS!

Town win Division Three title — and make history

Stan Hall reports on Town's night to remember

Shrewsbury, normally a "ghost" town on Thursday, was invaded by thousands of football crazy Town supporters yesterday for the crunch match with Exeter City which meant promotion to the Second Division for the first time for Shrewsbury Town Football Club in their 29 seasons in the Football League.

There were unprecedented scenes at the Gay Meadow at the final whistle as many of the record crowd for a league match this season invaded the pitch with shouts of "We are the champions," "We want the players" and "We want Graham Turner."

The players and their young player manager Graham Turner, who had been the first to acknowledge their triumph as they had made a hasty retreat to avoid the swarming supporters, responded to the supporters' cheers and chants by appearing in the directors box.

This was possibly the most emotional period in a season littered with emotion and drama, including those memorable FA Cup ties, climaxed by their first entry into the quarter-finals of the competition and their first competitive game against First Division Wolverhampton Wanderers at first team level.

Queues of fans, including many who had spent the day at the West-Mid Show, started to form an hour before kick-off time.

Thousands roamed the streets long after the end of the match, singing and chanting.

Public houses and clubs, mostly empty while the match was being played, began to fill quickly as supporters toasted the success of the club, in which they themselves had played no small part in recent weeks.

Last night was the climax to what has undoubtedly been the most exciting and involved finale to a Third Division season.

Watford, who gained so much publicity with their chairman Elton John, and Swansea, with their ex-Liverpool glamour stars, had their fate resolved in their last match of the season earlier in the week. Both have previously experienced Second Division football.

Shrewsbury made it a hat trick of teams knowing their fate with their last match. They had only to draw against Exeter to gain promotion; a win meant them going up as champions, their first ever since they entered the Football League 29 seasons ago.

With Swindon, also former Second Division material, having "blown" their chances with defeats on Saturday and Tuesday at Sheffield Wednesday — former Town player Brian Hornsby was one of the scorers — and Blackpool, the only other team in with a chance last night were Gillingham.

Gillingham entered the Football League the same season as Shrewsbury, and like them, have never been promoted to the Second. Ironically Gillingham supporters had celebrated their recent 2-0 home win against the Town as though they were already promoted. Now their last match of the season away to Chesterfield tomorrow afternoon is purely academic.

With a broad smile over his face, which has become almost a familiar sight on TV this season, Shrewsbury's young player-manager Graham Turner greeted promotion after the match when he told me: "I suppose relief is my first reaction because it has been so tense in recent weeks.

"But I am really going to enjoy the sweet flavour of the club's most successful season ever, when I have time to sit down alone and reflect on so many dramas in the six months since I took over.

"My immediate thought is for the players. Without them this feat would not have been possible and I am delighted for their sakes more than anyone else because they have worked so hard throughout the season.

"And I would also like to pay tribute to the supporters who have also played an important part in our success."

Club chairman Tim Yates told me promotion was a personal ambition fulfilled after 25 years on the board and exploded the myth that the board did not want promotion.

"Our thanks and congratulations are due to Graham Turner, who took over as manager after a good start to the season built by Richie Barker. To our players there is nothing but praise for the way they have worked this season."

Shrewsbury Town manager Graham Turner — relieved and delighted.

Ecstatic scenes of jubilation as Shrewsbury hammer their way into the Second Division —and the history books.

Original match programme of Shrewsbury's first home game in the Second Division: Shrewsbury 1 Notts County 1 (21 August 1979)

First Day cover issued to commemorate Shrewsbury's first home game in the Second Division

Manager Geoff Hurst, Clive Walker and members of the Chelsea ground staff in the dug-out. Shrewsbury 3 Chelsea 0 (15 September 1979)

Original match programme of Shrewsbury 3 Chelsea 0 (15 September 1979)

Autographed pictures of Clive Walker, Trevor Brooking and Frank Lampard obtained after victories over Chelsea and West Ham in 1979/80 season.

Shrewsbury Town players on Sun *Soccercards, including one obvious error – but it is definitely Jake!*

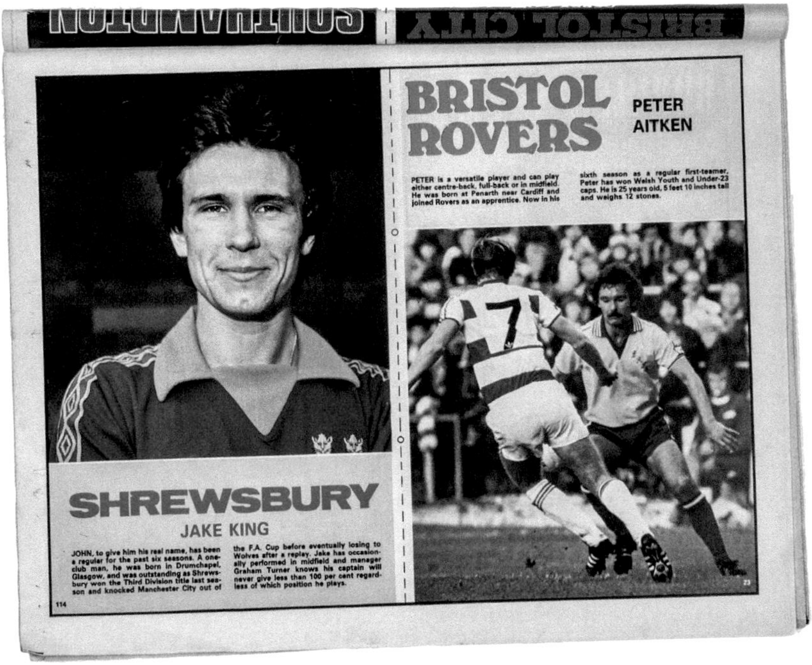

SOUTHAMPTON
BRISTOL CITY
BRISTOL ROVERS
PETER AITKEN
PETER is a versatile player and can play either centre-back, full-back or in midfield. He was born at Penarth near Cardiff and joined Rovers as an apprentice. Now in his sixth season as a regular first-teamer, Peter has won Welsh Youth and Under-23 caps. He is 25 years old, 5 feet 10 inches tall and weighs 12 stones.
SHREWSBURY
JAKE KING
JOHN, to give him his real name, has been a regular for the past six seasons. A one-club man, he was born in Drumchapel, Glasgow, and was outstanding as Shrewsbury won the Third Division title last season and knocked Manchester City out of the F.A. Cup before eventually losing to Wolves after a replay. Jake has occasionally performed in midfield and manager Graham Turner knows his captain will never give less than 100 per cent regardless of which position he plays.
114
23

Jake King profile and photo in Shoot!

SHREWSBURY TOWN
GAY MEADOW
FOOTBALL LEAGUE SECOND DIVISION
SUNDERLAND
ROKER PARK
SWANSEA CITY
VETCH FIELD
WATFORD
VICARAGE ROAD

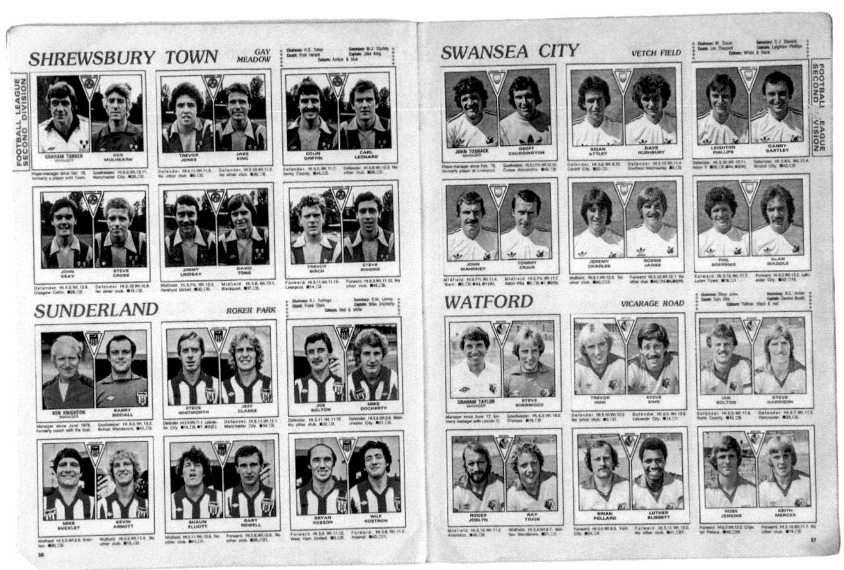

Shrewsbury Town Panini '80 stickers

Shrewsbury Town Transimage Football 79/80 sticker

EIGHT

M.A.B.
AUTO'S

Also —
LARGE STOCKS
OF
USED CARS

Queens Head 345
or
Oswestry 2656

A WINNING COMBINATION

KINGCUP
MmmmUSHROOMS
and Bacon for Sunday
Breakfast, or before
That Evening Game

Mushrooms and Bacon
a perfect match.

KINGCUP
MUSHROOMS Ltd.
of Hinstock, in Shropshire

FLETCHER (Contractors) LTD.
BUILDERS AND ESTATE DEVELOPERS

D.I.Y. & BUILDING MATERIALS

TIMBER, WALLBOARDS
PLYWOOD, GLASS, etc.
EXTENSIVE RANGE OF
PLASTER BOARD
ASBESTOS SHEET
Cut to Order — Very Competitive Prices

A. K. WILLIAMS
QUEEN STREET, MADELEY,
TELFORD.
TELEPHONE 585740

USE THAT FORGOTTEN LOFT SPACE
'Aleco' Loft Ladder

Home Sales Ladder Centre

FARR AND HARRIS LIMITED
(BUILDERS' AND PLUMBERS' MERCHANTS)

SHREWSBURY 3
NEWCASTLE 1

NINE

Travel

MAGNA THE
MAGNIFICENT

For Aggregates and Coated Materials
Sand & Gravel Readymixed Concrete
Surfacing Contracting

ARC Western

Amey Roadstone Corporation Limited

Telephone: Shrewsbury 6311 Telex: 35261

Insurance Brokers,
13/13a Dogpole,
Shrewsbury.

DBJ

Estate Agents
14 St Mary's Street,
Shrewsbury.

DAVIES BROWN & JENNINGS

(Incorporating A. & B.J. Estates)

C. EVANS & CO.
(Builders Merchants) LTD.

FOR ALL YOUR
BUILDING
MATERIALS

LONDON BRICK
THERMAL AND CONCRETE BLOCKS
PAVING, SCREEN BLOCKS ETC.
DRAINAGE BY HEPWORTH
BAT LINTELS AND PRODUCTS
CASTINGS
SAND AND CEMENT

Station Wharf, New Road,
MUCH WENLOCK
Telephone Much Wenlock
727118

OPEN 8.30-5.15 Daily.
8.30-12.30 Saturday

WHY HEAT
UNNECESSARY SPACE?

CUT HEAT LOSS
NOW!

INTERIOR DESIGN
CEILING CO. LTD.

VAN BEEK MOTOR COMPONENTS
DITHERINGTON ROAD — SHREWSBURY
TELEPHONE 67631 or 67632

Forty per cent discount on complete Exhaust Systems.

VAN BEEK MOTOR COMPONENTS

Section from Birmingham match programme showing victory over Newcastle in previous home game.

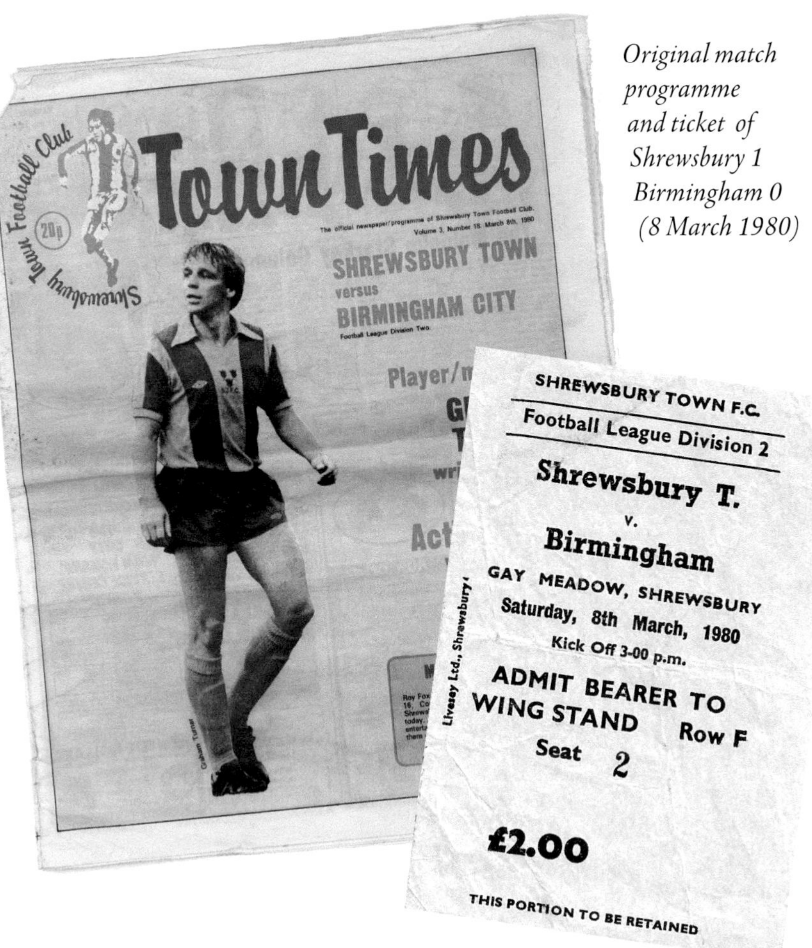

Shrewsbury Town Football Club

20p

Town Times

The official newspaper/programme of Shrewsbury Town Football Club. Volume 3, Number 18. March 8th, 1980

SHREWSBURY TOWN
versus
BIRMINGHAM CITY

Football League Division Two.

SHREWSBURY TOWN F.C.

Football League Division 2

Shrewsbury T.

v.

Birmingham

GAY MEADOW, SHREWSBURY

Saturday, 8th March, 1980

Kick Off 3-00 p.m.

ADMIT BEARER TO
WING STAND Row F
Seat 2

£2.00

THIS PORTION TO BE RETAINED

Livesey Ltd., Shrewsbury

Original match programme and ticket of Shrewsbury 1 Birmingham 0 (8 March 1980)

Performances by Shrewsbury players at home 79/80 Season

Teams / PLAYERS	Ken Mulhearn	Jake King	Carleton Leonard	Graham Turner	Colin Griffin	Jack Keay	Steve Cross	Ian Atkins	Dave Tong	Steve Biggins	Arthur Mann	Trevor Birch	Tony Larkin	Jimmy Lindsay	Sammy Chapman	Dean Edwards	Bob Wardle	Steve Hayes	John Dungworth	Paul Maguire	Coyne
Notts County	7	7½	7	7½	8	8	–	7	7	7½	8½	6½	–	–	–	–	–	–	–	–	–
Cambridge	7	7	–	5	7	8	6½	7	6	7½	7½	4	6	–	–	–	–	–	–	–	–
Chelsea	8½	7½	7	–	8	8	–	7½	8	8	7½	7½	–	8	–	–	–	–	–	–	–

Extract from player performance scores I'd given

Division 2

Luton	5	3	1	13	6	7
Newcastle	5	3	1	10	6	7
Leicester	5	3	1	11	5	7
Notts C	5	3	1	7	3	7
Sunderland	5	3	1	6	4	7
Preston	5	2	1	6	3	6
Bristol R	5	2	1	7	7	6
Wrexham	5	3	2	7	7	6
Cardiff	5	3	2	5	6	6
Swansea	5	2	1	5	7	6
Chelsea	5	2	2	4	5	5
Watford	5	1	1	5	5	5
B'ham C	5	2	2	8	9	5
Cambridge	5	1	1	6	7	5
Fulham	5	2	2	6	8	5
Q.P.R.	5	2	3	6	6	4
Oldham	5	1	3	8	8	3
Burnley	5	0	2	5	7	3
West Ham	5	1	3	2	5	3
Orient	5	0	2	5	9	3
Charlton	5	0	2	4	8	3
Shrewsbury	5	0	4	3	8	1

*Division Two table after five games. Shrewsbury 22nd (*Town Times *programme v Chelsea, 15 September 1979)*

DIVISION TWO
up to and including Saturday, May 3rd
1980

					Goals					Goals		
	P	W	D	L	F	A	W	D	L	F	A	Ps
Leicester	42	12	5	4	32	19	9	8	4	26	19	55
Birmingham	42	14	5	2	37	16	7	6	8	21	22	53
Chelsea	42	14	3	4	34	16	9	4	8	32	36	53
Sunderland	41	15	5	0	45	13	5	7	9	22	29	52
QPR	42	10	9	2	46	25	8	4	9	29	28	49
Luton	42	9	10	2	36	17	7	7	7	30	28	49
West Ham	40	12	2	6	33	20	7	5	8	17	20	45
Cambridge	42	11	6	4	40	23	3	10	8	21	30	44
Newcastle	42	13	6	2	35	19	2	8	11	18	30	44
Preston	42	8	10	3	30	23	4	9	8	26	29	43
Oldham	42	12	5	4	30	21	4	6	11	19	32	43
Swansea	42	13	1	7	31	20	4	8	9	17	33	43
Shrewsbury	42	12	3	6	41	23	6	2	13	19	30	41
Orient	42	7	9	5	29	31	5	8	8	19	23	41
Cardiff	42	11	4	6	21	16	5	4	12	20	32	40
Wrexham*	42	13	2	6	26	15	3	4	14	14	34	38
Notts Cnty	42	4	11	6	24	22	7	4	10	27	30	37
Watford	42	9	6	6	27	18	3	7	11	12	28	37
Bristol R	42	9	8	4	33	23	2	5	14	17	41	35
Fulham	42	6	4	11	19	28	5	3	13	23	46	29
Burnley	42	5	9	7	19	23	1	6	14	20	50	27
Charlton	41	6	6	9	25	31	0	4	16	13	43	22

*Division Two table after 42 games. Shrewsbury 13th (*Town Times *programme v Newport, 12 May 1980)*

Shrewsbury 1 Orient 0
Biggins
Not a very good game but at least Salop got both points.
6,176

Shrewsbury 2 Leicester 2
Chapman, King Goodwin, [illegible]
A very exciting game with a good atmosphere. Salop took the lead in the 1st half from Chapman but in the 2nd half Mark Goodwin scored a brilliant 25 yard drive, it was a great goal. This gave Leicester added incentive and soon after they scored another from Pat Byrne. But about 15 minutes from the end Jake King scored with a header and thats how the scoreline remained.
9,045

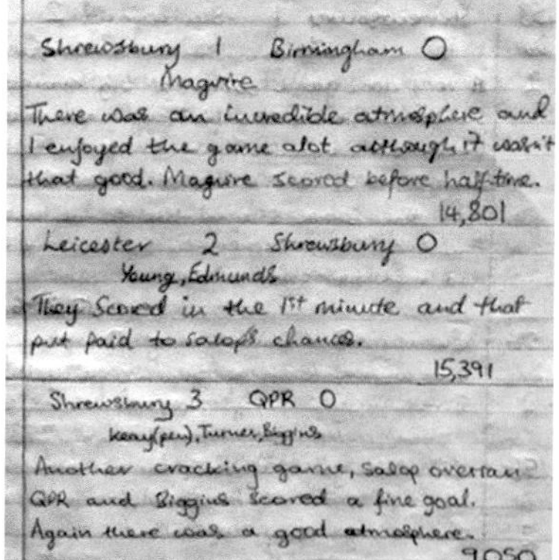
Shrewsbury 1 Birmingham 0
Maguire
There was an incredible atmosphere and I enjoyed the game alot although it wasn't that good. Maguire scored before half-time.
14,801

Leicester 2 Shrewsbury 0
Young, Edmunds
They scored in the 1st minute and that put paid to Salop's chances.
15,391

Shrewsbury 3 QPR 0
Kenny (pen), Turner, Biggins
Another cracking game, Salop overran QPR and Biggins scored a fine goal. Again there was a good atmosphere.
9,050

Extracts from my 'Matches I've been to' diary

Aerial view of Gay Meadow

fans) about targets. Two specific aims were outlined in his column: retaining the Welsh Cup and keeping clear of the bottom eight places in order to gain exemption from the first round of the League Cup for the following season. The incentives were evident but only one of the objectives was met, and in the grander scheme of things, it was the one that was more significant – finishing close to the mid-point of the Second Division carried more prestige than another Welsh Cup victory.

Home Matchday 20
'Turn it on again'

A 0-0 draw at Luton was a creditable result for Shrewsbury and had probably ended the Hatters' promotion aspirations. The penultimate home game of the season against Oldham Athletic was approaching and although Town had lost five games at Gay Meadow, we were the only team in the Football League to have scored in every home match up to this point, so it would be good to maintain that record. Getting another win under the belt against mid-table opposition was the realistic objective. And if the contest was half as exciting as the midweek Welsh Cup semi-final second leg clash with Swansea, which Town had won on penalties after drawing 2-2 on aggregate, the fans would be going home happy.

19 April 1980
Shrewsbury Town 0 Oldham 1
Attendance: 6,862

Saturday wasn't just football day, Saturday was *Tiswas* day. Although I'd been as excited as any other 12-year-old when the BBC's *Multi-Coloured Swapshop* was launched in 1976, my teenage tastes had developed and (im)matured so I'd switched allegiance to the anarchic mayhem now being broadcast on ATV. How could you not be drawn to the live entertainment served up by presenter Chris Tarrant and a motley crew of regulars: the Phantom Flan Flinger, Trevor McDoughnut and Spit the Dog? It's possible that others were lured in by the sultry charm of co-presenter Sally James in her leather waistcoat. Oh matron. Whatever took your fancy, it was hard to take your eyes off the on-screen carnage for fear of missing a moment of hilarity or a wince-inducing mishap, usually involving a flan or bucket of slime and an upset child.

On Sundays I always tuned into another Midlands TV show, *Star Soccer*, a little more sedate than *Tiswas* but equally required viewing. Hosted by Gary Newbon, the programme aired matches featuring local teams with commentary by Hugh Johns. In the 1979/80 season, Forest, Wolves, Villa and WBA all finished in the First Division's top ten so there was no shortage of quality footy footage. After being promoted, Shrewsbury even got a bit more televisual coverage on *Star Soccer* (that wasn't hard), as part of the 'Second Division specials'.

According to my diary, this very day had started promisingly. I'd chortled at *Tiswas* and full of the joys of spring, headed off to watch Salop beat Oldham. The away team's winning goal was scored by Simon Stainrod, the best player on the pitch that day (though he didn't have much competition). Shrewsbury didn't score and my concise match report amounted to six words, 'The worst game of the season!' I'd been even more succinct in my personal diary, 'It was shit.' Moving on.

For an avid teenage football fan, an added bonus of Second Division status was your team getting more exposure in the football press and in magazines such as *Shoot!* and *Match*, but perhaps the crowning glory was seeing mugshots of the team in Panini's *Football '80* sticker collection. The first warning signs of this particular addiction had emerged in the early 70s when I was introduced to *The Wonderful World of Soccer Stars* albums including their World Cup 1974 edition. As well as seeking to complete these collections, my habit was fuelled by other football cards issued by companies such as Topps and Barratt. The small, pinkish, rectangular sticks of bubble gum that came with some packets were tasteless and unchewable and some sets of cards didn't even seem to have albums available to fill. I didn't really care. I still wanted the cards. Needed them. In the early to middle part of the decade, I was almost out of control and bingeing on break-time swapping frenzies at school, my jacket pockets containing bundles of stickers held together by rubber bands. Got got got. Need. Got. I had hundreds of the damn things and must have spent a small fortune on them. I'm over it now. Oh yes. Not a problem any more. Haven't touched a Panini sticker in years. All in the past. Finito. Unless anyone's got a spare Gustavo de Simone of Uruguay (number 227) from that 1974 World Cup collection?

In *Football '80*, as Second Division clubs, each team only got half a page and two players shared one sticker, but heck, Town were in the album (with Sunderland placed below). We'd made it! The player-manager and familiar faces from the first team line-up were clad in the classic blue-and-amber-striped shirts with the loggerheads on the club crests just showing. Most were smiling or at least attempting to. The full beam beneath Colin Griffin's 'tache was rather disarming. Colin never did that on the pitch.

And hold on a minute! Where's Acker? Where's Maguire? Two of Shrewsbury's stars were missing. Maybe injuries had kept them away from the photo shoot. Maybe they'd gone AWOL. Trevor Birch was in. Fair enough – he made a few appearances over the season and had scored a few useful goals. But who the devil was Trevor Jones? 'Defender. Ht 5.11. Wt. 11.5. No other club. Appearances 0. Goals 0.' He didn't play for the club that season or it seems, any other season. But he still got himself on a Panini football sticker, you lucky, lucky, non-playing defender. He wasn't even smiling. In another album from that time, Transimage's *Football 79/80*, 15 miniature mugshots of Shrewsbury players appeared on one sticker. It was nice to see that Town stood out, as all the other Second Division stickers featured teeny weeny, pretty little, pretty pointless team shots.

Against Oldham, one of the few players who again produced an above-average shift, according to my player rankings, was David Tong. The energetic, attacking midfielder had been an integral part of the Third Division championship-winning campaign after joining Town from Blackpool. Tong appeared in every league game during 1979/80 but had donned jerseys with different numbers on the back – 4, 7, 8, 9, 11 and 12 (just once). Jack Keay, another fine young player, was the only Town player to start every game that season. A tremendous achievement (scoring 20 goals for Salop over the years was no mean feat either). Tong's youthful good looks hinted at an alternative or parallel career in a mid-70s boyband such as Flintlock, or maybe Child? I loved his marauding runs down the right side of the pitch, which often ended with a pinpoint cross or a long-range shot. He was far from prolific in terms of goals scored but was still a vital member of the team and very popular with the Gay Meadow faithful.

But the smiles seen in Panini's *Football '80* sticker collection were not evident on the players' faces at the end of the Oldham game. Same for the home fans too. The performance had been poor. The feat of being the only league team to score in every home game had gone. Town were now in 16th place. Two games to go. Safe from relegation. Next up was West Ham away – it wasn't worth thinking about completing the double over the other big London club, as we'd done with Chelsea, was it? Nothing to lose though. Let's turn it on again at Upton Park!

Home Matchday 21
'Talk of the Town'

Fittingly, the main man was on the front cover of *Town Times* for the last league game of the season. A grinning Graham Turner in cool-looking track top was proudly holding a huge bottle of Bell's Whisky aloft after winning the Manager of the Month award for March. This achievement crowned the campaign's golden period which had started in February with Town going on to win six consecutive games, enjoying victories over Chelsea and Wrexham away and Newcastle and Birmingham at home, in a crazy, beautiful five-week period. The Shrewsbury boss had earned all the plaudits for steering the club to a commendable 14th in the table before this final fixture. A win in this last match could conceivably result in an even higher placing.

3 May 1980
Shrewsbury Town 5 Fulham 2
Attendance: 6,328

Turner had nearly 300 games under his belt for Wrexham and Chester before he made the move to Shropshire in 1973. He topped that total by making over 350 appearances for Shrewsbury, but there was more to come off the field. Much more. In late 1978 he had become Town's player-manager, leading them to Third Division championship glory and into the Second Division for the first time in the club's history (sorry, have I already mentioned that?) After four more seasons at this level, including an eighth-place finish, the club's highest ever, Turner went on to manage Aston Villa. He later had a more successful run at Wolves and then Hereford, before returning to Shrewsbury in 2010 and achieving another promotion. That £30,000 transfer fee paid to Chester City back in 1973 must be one of the best bits of business ever done by the club.

In the penultimate fixture of 1979/80, Shrewsbury would be playing a league game at Upton Park for the first time. West Ham had recently beaten Everton in an epic FA Cup semi-final (the one when Frank Lampard senior celebrated his winning goal by dancing round the corner flag) so it was perhaps understandable that the coat pocket-sized *Hammer* programme devoted considerable coverage to their imminent trip to Wembley. All credit to the illustrious East End club, though, as the programme also proclaimed, 'It is a pleasure as well as a notable event to welcome this afternoon's visitors.' The feature then mentioned that the Shrews' reserves had played at Upton Park in 1965 and lost 9-1. It also suggested that the home team now had 'the opportunity to avenge the 3-0 defeat' at the Meadow back in December. Not gonna happen. Town registered a surprising, but hugely impressive, 3-1 away win. Maguire and a Keay penalty made the difference at half-time with Biggins getting a third to stun the crowd of 19,765, apart from the elated Salopian travelling support. Brooking scored for West Ham and would do so again when his team beat Arsenal 1-0 in the FA Cup Final a week after the season's league fixtures had ended.

Although Turner had played in the match at Upton Park and had featured in most other games for Town over the campaign, he would not appear against Fulham. As he admitted in his column for the programme, the manager was already preparing for next season, and had planned a scouting mission to Scotland to watch a Premier Division striker. The gaffer was looking ahead, hoping to stock up on supplies for the coming months. The 'Deep Freeze' feature in the programme also promoted forward thinking as local butchers across the county (from Bishop's Castle, Bridgnorth, Church Stretton, Shrewsbury and Telford) encouraged potential customers to select their finest quality meat products and stick them in the freezer. There didn't seem to be any evidence of vegetarian options.

In the programme, club secretary Malcolm Starkey was also eager to thank fans for supporting the club and was pleased about the 'excellent average' for attendances at Gay Meadow. After 21 home league games, the figure stood at approximately 8,750, quite a bit more than the 8,000 hoped for. The player-manager felt that most fans would have 'little cause for complaint' about the standard of entertainment offered at the ground during the first campaign at this level. Apart from the Oldham game, I couldn't argue with that view and the final match served up the biggest goal-fest of the season. Biggins,

Keay (pen), Dungworth and King were on target for Town, while already-relegated Fulham contributed an own goal to the home tally, as well as getting a couple on the scoresheet too. My account of the seven-goal thriller was summed up thus, 'This game wasn't as exciting as it sounds but it was pretty good all the same.' A career following in the footsteps of Brian Glanville didn't seem likely. The two points took Shrewsbury up to 13th position, a notable achievement in itself, and one which would give the club a bye in the first round of the League Cup in August.

The 21 home games offered by my £12 junior season ticket had yielded incredible value in my eyes. On page two of *Town Times* for the last league game, prices for 1980/81 season tickets were presented. The rates had gone up. I was no longer a junior and I didn't renew.

Over the season, based on my individual performance grades for each home game, the overall winner of my own prestigious player of the year award was David Tong with an impressive average score of 7.35, closely followed by Ian 'Acker' Atkins. I was pleased that the Town supporters reached the same verdict, voting the 'hard-working midfielder' their star man too. I even compiled a Second Division opponents team of the players who had most impressed me at the Meadow:

1. Chris Turner (Sunderland)
2. Ray Stewart (West Ham)
3. Mark Dennis (Birmingham)
4. Glenn Roeder (QPR)
5. Larry May (Leicester)
6. Paul Price (Luton)
7. Steve Fox (Leicester)
8. David Moss (Luton)
9. Steve Elliot (Preston)
10. Tony Currie (QPR)
11. Stan Cummins (Middlesbrough)
12. Alan Brown (Sunderland)

Town now had the Welsh Cup in their sights but needed to overcome a 2-1 first leg deficit against Newport County. Losing the home return 3-0 was a bit of an anti-climax.

But that wasn't a loss to be dwelt upon. As Turner re-emphasised in his parting column for the season before the Welsh Cup Final second leg, the club had achieved the target of finishing clear of the bottom eight and pointed out, 'In effect the Town players earned themselves an extra week's holiday.' The boss didn't gush about the team's achievements over the season, but as ever remained focused, outlining some impending administrative duties and his ongoing desire to strengthen the squad in preparation for the next campaign. Turner did mention his hopes of getting a family vacation in Scotland – perhaps with a bit of talent scouting thrown in! He certainly deserved a break – as did the players, who, like the previous summer, could look forward to the beach, the sun, the sea and the sangria.

Town's first season in the Second Division warranted celebration and it was editor Bryan Pritchard who expressed it most clearly by championing the fact that Shrewsbury had exceeded most people's expectations, particularly after such an indifferent start. He commended the manager on staying calm and keeping faith in his team. He singled out key moments such as taking four points off West Ham but also said, 'There have been many games this season that will be remembered by supporters for many years to come for one reason or another.'

Spot on, Bryan, and we'd played our part by roaring our team on in convincing home victories over Chelsea, West Ham, Newcastle, QPR and Wrexham as well as the narrow win against Birmingham. We'd held eventual Second Division champions Leicester to a 2-2 draw. All these spectacles had been played out in front of large, fervent Gay Meadow crowds. We'd witnessed our Shropshire club's inaugural league game in the second tier, and cheered in delight at Colin Griffin's first goal for the side at this level. Let's not bring up Oldham again (oops). Overall, the team had performed magnificently but special credit had to go to one man, the player-manager: arise Lord Turner of Salop.

Make no mistake, these were good times. It had been an outstanding season following Town. There wouldn't be any more football for a while but 'Geno' by Dexy's Midnight Runners had hit the top of the charts, The Cure had just released 'A Forest' and in exactly two Saturdays' time, I had tickets to see The Undertones at Malvern Winter Gardens. Happy days.

4

Peaks, highs, and very low lows

ALTHOUGH I didn't renew my season ticket that summer, I was there for the opening game in 1980/81, a 1-1 draw against Grimsby Town. I was also at the following home fixture against Chelsea. Clive Walker did start in this one; he showed his panache and scored in the 2-2 draw. In January 1981 I was back for an FA Cup third round game, as recounted in my diary, 'Met some mates at The Radbrook. Had four pints and two vodkas, went down to the Meadow, pretty pissed, good laugh and saw Salop draw 0-0 with Ipswich. Came home, had a headache and watched *The Professionals*.' It wasn't big. It wasn't clever. It's what we did as callow youths. It's a bit embarrassing looking back now.

For the next couple of years while I was still living in South Shropshire, my Saturday routine changed. Instead of watching live football at Shrewsbury, I was now playing regular football for the Bishop's Castle B team. This was probably about level 273 in the pyramid, but it did have its moments. As a consequence, from a Town-supporting perspective, in 1981/82 I missed impressive wins over the likes of Derby and Palace. And while Shrewsbury were beating Ipswich 2-1 in the fifth round of another famous FA Cup run, I was attempting, not always successfully, to perform a Hansen-like, ball-playing centre-back role as the BC B team won 5-4 at Stoke Rovers. And when Shrewsbury were valiantly exiting the cup in the quarter-final at Leicester City (5-2), I was slipping around a muddy pitch 'in monsoon conditions' but helping to stuff Springvale 4-1. I still really have no idea where those football teams are located. I played for Bishop's Castle first team too and in my first game, away at fierce local rivals, with minutes remaining, I curled a delightful shot round the onrushing keeper to score the winner. Unhappily for me, it was an own goal and I was never picked again.

I did still take trips to Shrewsbury around this time but mostly on Friday nights – we'd discovered the Crystal Goblet club, a room above Tiffanys, where we'd throw weird shapes on the small dancefloor to the sounds of The B52s, Echo and the Bunnymen and Joy Division. Attempting to dance to Bauhaus' Bela Lugosi's Dead was a step too far but we did admire the young goths who were up for that challenge.

Amazingly, Town retained their Second Division status for nine more seasons after their debut appearance, with further commendable rankings in the table during that period, including record finishes of eighth in consecutive seasons, 1983/84 and 1984/85. Not bad for a small town in Shropshire. Relegation from the second tier in English football happened at the end of the 1988/89 season. Town haven't been back since.

Unfortunately, I didn't witness much of this first-hand, as I'd headed off to university in 1983 which led to a lengthy hiatus in my visits to Gay Meadow. I still followed Town, but from afar, as an exiled Shrew, based at different times in Leeds, Thessaloniki, London, Heraklion, Wrocław and Kuala Lumpur. In my separation period, my lost years, I heard stories of more home wins against Chelsea, the 5-1 demolition of Leeds, and a narrow League Cup quarter-final defeat by Southampton. It was a shame not to have been among the 472 folk who were there to see the 10-0 Welsh Cup win over Cefn Albion in 1986.

My absence stretched into the 1990s. I was missing in action (living overseas) for the club's first Wembley appearance in the 1996 Football League Trophy Final, when Rotherham won 2-1 with Nigel Jemson scoring both goals. A few years later the same player would be wearing a blue-and-amber-striped shirt and would score the winner in one of Town's greatest ever victories. I was also away for the Great Escape at Exeter in May 2000, when Mickey Brown's deciding goal staved off relegation from the Football League.

Since the early 21st century, though, I've been based in Kenilworth, Warwickshire, and my reacquaintance with Town in that period has seen a fair share of ups and downs, so let's start with the final few years at Gay Meadow. By this time, former Everton centre-back Kevin Ratcliffe was now in charge and Luke Rodgers was banging in the goals up front. There was a play-off near miss in 2001/02 and things seemed to be looking up. Little did we know that the following season was going to be one hell of a big dipper ride that would not end well.

2002/03

High highs and very low lows

In the early stages of the FA Cup, I'd driven over to watch Shrewsbury cruise past Stafford Rangers (4-0) and Barrow (3-1) before the landing of a plummier tie, against Everton in the third round. The Premier League team were having a great season and lying fifth in the table. Town were in 86th position in the football pyramid and had recently lost 6-0 to Boston and 5-1 to Rushden & Diamonds. This game would be a welcome distraction from the league and financially rewarding but there weren't too many expectations of it being much of a contest. Nevertheless, there is always a slim chance of an upset and the match-up also neatly ticked some other 'romance of the cup' boxes: Ratcliffe would be facing his former team, who he had captained to FA Cup success in 1984, while ex-Town skipper David Moyes was now managing the Toffees.

Adding even more spice to the occasion was the prospect of a 17-year-old football sensation coming to the Meadow. A few weeks earlier, at 16, the teenage prodigy had scored a stunning last-minute winner against Arsenal with commentator Clive Tyldesley roaring, 'Remember the name: Waaaaayne Rooney.' In December, the player was voted BBC Young Sports Personality of the Year. Even at such a tender age, this wasn't Rooney's first appearance at Shrewsbury's ground; that had been a 20-minute run out in a pre-season friendly, with the visitors strolling to a 3-0 win. Yet, even with all these tasty-looking ingredients, the match still hadn't been selected as one of the live cup games to be shown on the BBC.

In the third round of January 2003, the Evertonians weren't given a chance to stroll, and completely blew their chance to win the game. And it wasn't a teenager who made the headlines but instead a 33-year-old seasoned pro. Nigel Jemson had been in the limelight before, tasting success after scoring the only goal for Nottingham Forest in the 1990 League Cup Final but now seemed to be winding down his career at his 12th league club. He wasn't done though. On 38 minutes, Jemson curled a majestic free kick over the wall for the opening goal and the chant of 'Are you watching, BBC?' burst out around the ground. Although substitute Niclas Alexandersson equalised in the second half to provide a reality check, in the dying moments, the veteran popped up again to glance in a near-post header from a set piece delivered by Ian Woan, sending those of us in the Wakeman End and three-quarters of Gay Meadow absolutely bonkers.

Yes, a replay at Goodison would have been extremely lucrative for the club – it's natural for a lower-league chairman to think that – but 'fanthink' is usually different, 'Some more funds to invest? Hmmm, let me see, no, on balance we'll take the ecstasy, the giant-killing glory, the memories, if you don't mind.' The performance of 'Precious Jem' (the next day's headline in the *Sunday Times*) and his Town team-mates that day, masterminded by Ratcliffe, gave us all those elements. Everton's boy wonder got a few pelters from the locals and was booked for dissent. Commendably, Rooney did leave his shirt to be auctioned for charity and at least got his photo on the front of the *Harka* match programme, but even then, his striker counterpart on the cover, Town's very own short-haired, shortish, combative young terrier, Luke Rodgers, completely upstaged him on the pitch. Rooney would go on to have better days. For Shrewsbury Town Football Club, days don't get much better than that one.

The Beeb did decide to bring its cameras and crew to the Meadow to do a live broadcast for the fourth round tie. Town had been drawn against Chelsea, who were fourth in the Premier League. The quality of the team they put out on that Sunday evening in late January is worth highlighting as it included Carlo Cudicini, William Gallas, John Terry, Frank Lampard, World Cup winner Emmanuel Petit, Boudewijn Zenden and Graeme Le Saux. The Town line-up to face these giants was: Ian Dunbavin, Darren Moss, David Artell, Peter Wilding, Alex Smith, Steve Jagielka, Jamie Tolley, Mark Atkins, Ian Woan, Luke Rodgers and Nigel Jemson. Substitutes Leon Drysdale, Ryan Lowe and Karl Murray all made appearances too. But of all the players who ran around the pitch that night, one player stood out. In his match report for the *Daily Telegraph* (27 January 2003), Henry Winter articulated it perfectly, 'The twinkling feet of Gianfranco Zola still possess the power to bewitch. At 36, age has not withered Zola's sumptuous gifts, merely lent him further wisdom in how to impose them so tellingly.'

Again, we stood at the Wakeman End, not cheering wildly this time but in awe of the Italian footballing superhero at the centre of everything, watching him score two cracking goals and crossing for Carlton Cole to head in another. Jody Morris curled in the fourth. There had been absolutely no chance of a cup upset on this occasion. Defeat was certainly no disgrace and the club had pocketed considerable funds from their FA Cup run, including TV fees. And as aficionados of the beautiful game, we had been lucky enough to witness a wonderful individual performance. At the end of his piece, Winter summed it up brilliantly, 'And so the curtain was brought down on Shrewsbury Town's fairytale, but the magic of Zola lives on.' Cheers Henry. Couldn't have put it better myself.

The rest of the season was not a fairytale. On 1 February, the first league game after bowing out of the cup, Town got a useful point away at Exeter and were seventh from bottom with a game or two in hand on all the teams below. A month later, Shrewsbury beat Rochdale 3-1 and remained in 18th place. But then the rot set in. There were no more wins in March and by 5 April Town had dropped to 21st after a 0-0 home draw against Swansea City. Town had 41 points and still had more games to play than those below, with eight left. In the next fixture, it was depressing enough to lose at home to local rivals Wrexham but the fans were still clinging on to a sliver of hope that the dreaded drop could be avoided. Exeter were at the foot of the table at this point having played two games more. Did Town have a Great Escape 2 card up their sleeves in emergency? Could we parachute Mickey Brown in to save the day again? The rot did not stop and soon became a collapse of catastrophic proportions, with further defeats by Darlington, Macclesfield Town, Boston United, Bournemouth and Hartlepool placing us firmly at the bottom of the form table, as shown in the programme for the Carlisle game, the penultimate fixture of the 2002/03 season. Even more distressingly, Town were now anchored at the bottom of the real Third Division table.

In his 'Team Talk' feature in the Carlisle programme for that evening game on 29 April 2003, Kevin Ratcliffe cut to the chase, 'It's now or never then tonight as we enter the point of no return where nothing else than a win will be enough to keep alive our hopes of staying up.' It didn't take long to discover that it was the 'never' option that would be activated so Town shot down the chute to the Conference. Rodgers converted a penalty to give a glimmer of hope but that was soon extinguished by two quick goals by the visitors in response and a third just after half-time. Even though Rodgers pulled one back just before the end, Shrewsbury's 53 years in the Football League were over. Carlisle's hat-trick hero was Brian Wake and as the supporters filed quietly out of Gay Meadow that night, that surname seemed to capture the mood. Ratcliffe resigned the next day. According to a *Shropshire Star* poll, Steve Cotterill was a popular choice to succeed him, but Mark Atkins took on the caretaker role for the final league game against Scunthorpe. Town lost that too, the eighth consecutive defeat. It had been a sorry end to a season, which had encapsulated the extreme highs and lows of supporting a lower league team. Participating in the Conference in 2003/04 would present new experiences and take Shrewsbury Town to unfamiliar destinations to face teams such as Farnborough Town and Northwich Victoria.

2003/04

A year in the Conference

In this section I'd love to be able to recount interesting away days to obscure footballing locations up and down the country: trips to Woking, to Gravesend & Northfleet, to Leigh RMI (Railway Mechanics Institute); to describe encounters with old friends and foes like Chester, Aldershot and Exeter; or to analyse the two M54 derbies with our Shropshire neighbours Telford (they didn't go well). But I can't as I wasn't there and I'm sorry. I'm going to cite family and work commitments at the time, with an unhealthy dose of apathy and disillusionment thrown in too. I'm going to come clean: a two-and-a-half-hour round trip to watch Tamworth on a Sunday just didn't float my boat.

But then again, one occasion that season was the exception to the rule. It wasn't the play-off semi-final first leg against Barnet, which I watched on my own in a Kenilworth pub, narrowly avoiding a contretemps with a local rude mechanical who wanted to switch channels and watch the darts. Nor was it the second leg, which Town edged on away goals. It wasn't even the nerve-wrangling play-off final victory over Aldershot on penalties at Stoke City's Britannia Stadium. On that day I had made an earlier commitment to be at a significant family celebration, so was confined to following the game surreptitiously on the radio and via the internet. No, the big occasion was my 40th birthday in November 2003. I'd already been to the Camp Nou so that option was out. Watching David Beckham at the Bernabéu Stadium in La Liga was considered but a much better option, as stated on my invitation card, was 'Luke at the Gay Meadow in the Vauxhall Conference'.

I was a bit behind the times: it was now the Nationwide Conference.

Apart from the cost and logistics of organising this important event, another influential factor in the decision was the fact that Hereford United were the opponents so it was a top-of-the-table local derby. And in charge of the visitors was the legendary Graham Turner. Perfect! I decided that the occasion was worth splashing out on and celebrating in style, so we went for the 'special package' which marketing manager Mike Thomas confirmed in a letter. For £35 a head (including VAT), we would get the following:

* One ticket per person in the stands
* Lunch in the players' lounge including some wine
* A programme each
* A mention in the programme
* Parking if necessary

The bar bill would be extra.

This seemed very reasonable so on 22 November my dad, brother and six mates headed to Shrewsbury from different parts of the country. As we took our seats in the surprisingly small and pretty crammed Arthur Rowley Players' Lounge and began to add to the bar bill, any illusions my guests might have had that this 'package' would involve fine dining in an exclusive, luxurious setting, were instantly dispelled. Welcome to Gay Meadow! Lunch was served up: beef stroganoff or veggie burgers. Haute cuisine it was not. It didn't matter as tales of Town matches of yore were told and the complimentary wine flowed; well, we had a glass each. Matchday programmes were distributed and yes, there was a mention of our visit, under the list of match sponsors. We were given a nicely laid out team sheet – bonus! Luke Rodgers was on the bench. I was presented with a signed match ball by Chic Bates. One of my mates still goes on about how awestruck I looked. He's not wrong – what a moment! I didn't need to ask for Chic's autograph as I already had at least four of those in my collection.

After paying our bar bill and in good spirits, we made our way up to the back of the stands and took our seats. It looked like a decent crowd, with the Station End to our right housing a large away following. My pessimistic side was telling me that this most excellent day so far would probably be marred by a 0-0 draw, or a defeat. I needn't have worried.

There was a brilliant atmosphere in the ground and at 6,585, it was the highest attendance for a Conference game so far that season. The home side didn't let me (or my guests) down, spectacularly rising to the occasion.

Martin O'Connor and Colin Cramb shot Town into a 2-0 lead by the break. Kevin Street and Duane Darby added to the rout, before a late consolation reply from the visitors. Even my non-Shrewsbury-supporting mates were up off their seats, roaring their approval. Stuart Dunn, the 'Voice of Shrewsbury Town', in his report for the *Non-League Paper*, recounted how manager Jimmy Quinn described it as 'our best performance of the season'. It had been the perfect Gay Meadow/Shrewsbury Town package – £35 (including Vat) very well spent. Still buzzing, we set off to Bishop's Castle, where we spent the rest of the evening drinking the Three Tuns pub's home-brewed ale.

5

Back in the Football League

AFTER THE joys of the play-off final triumph, there was still an unmistakeable buzz about the place as Town returned to the newly named League Two, with the Football League now sponsored by Coca-Cola. I was buzzing enough to be there for the opener against Lincoln City. On the cover of the matchday programme, manager Jimmy Quinn was holding the Nationwide Conference play-off trophy aloft. Optimism coursed through the pages of that edition but captain Darren Tinson stressed that it was a priority to consolidate. The boss also sounded a note of caution, saying that it would be tough and adding, 'At the end of the day it's about winning. Everybody is happy when you're winning and everyone is unhappy when you lose, and I am certainly unhappy when we lose.'

Shrewsbury lost 1-0 and then went on to be beaten in three more of their first five league games. Everyone was unhappy, and the manager was certainly unhappy. The board were particularly unhappy as the form did not improve much and Quinn was gone by October. His replacement, Gary Peters, did ultimately manage to retain the club's league status but not without some squeaky bum time along the way. There was excitement that season – my dad and I enjoyed a six-goal thriller (4-2 v Kidderminster Harriers, from 2-0 down) but also suffered some pretty dire fare too (0-0 v Cambridge). Well, I suppose you could call finishing fourth from bottom consolidation of a sort.

2005/06

Young guns

Two young local players were establishing themselves and making an impact. Joe Hart, the Shrewsbury-born keeper, was getting rave reviews for his performances between the sticks. Unfortunately his penalty taking wasn't of the same standard. In a League Cup tie against Championship high-fliers Sheffield United, he had made a string of brilliant saves but then completely botched the deciding spot kick and Town were out.

Hart would soon get a move to Manchester City, go on loan to Birmingham, and then return to the City of Manchester Stadium. He went on to represent England 75 times. At the 2016 Euros in Saint-Étienne before his appearance against Slovakia, my old school-mate Griff and I would pose for a photo in front of a huge St George's flag with the words 'Shrewsbury Town', 'Pride', 'Passion', 'Belief' and 'Floreat Salopia'.

The other Shropshire starlet was Dave Edwards, and in the Leyton Orient programme in March, he featured in a double-page centre spread, cutting a casually cool pose in turquoise Adidas hoody, hands thrust in the pockets of his fashionable-looking jeans. His contributions on the pitch were garnering attention too and he scored the second goal in a 3-3 draw that day. It looked like the young lad from Pontesbury had potential, which could also be said of the team as a whole; finishing tenth was a marked improvement.

2006/07
Goodbye Gay Meadow

Everyone knew that leaving the old ground at the end of the season would be emotional, but little did we know that our emotions would be tested to extremes at a rather more grandiose stadium to conclude the campaign. I was making efforts to get to more home games now and my final tally was nine. My strike rate for wins wasn't great: drew five, lost three with a sole victory, 4-2 over Stockport County on 1 January. Despite not witnessing many winning performances, the team were churning them out and went on a 14-match unbeaten run to put them in contention for a place in the play-offs, which they could secure in the last league game of the season, in the final league fixture at Gay Meadow.

And it turned out to be quite a day. There had been tremendous demand to watch the match against Grimsby Town so I felt lucky and privileged when I was handed my ticket at the main office (I had been worried that it would get lost in the post). I bought the 132-page 'End of an Era' commemorative programme which had been produced for the occasion. At £10, it was a fitting memento. Reverting to schoolboy mode and lurking near the main entrance, I was able to get Gary Peters to sign my copy. Naturally, I got the T-shirt. It remains unworn and in the attic. In a moment of madness and going against my principles on such matters, I bought a Shrewsbury–Grimsby half-and-half scarf as the uniqueness and rarity of this item simply cried out to my obsessive collector nature – stick that up next to your Manchester United–Barcelona version! The following week I even ordered one of the specially commissioned paintings of the final game, signed by the squad. This was memorabilia from heaven.

On that sunny afternoon in May, supporters flocked into the ground and it was packed by 2pm, with an impressive turnout of Mariners fans squeezed into the

Station End. I took my place in the Wakeman End, five or six rows from the front. We were treated to a parade of former Shrewsbury players walking slowly round the edge of the pitch, clearly revelling in another day in the Salopian sun, stopping for the odd photo and signing autographs. I picked my target, my moment and lurched forward towards the low wall. Result: a treasured snap of me in a vintage blue and amber Town shirt next to the legend that is Steve Biggins, smartly decked out in jacket and tie, shades and name badge.

And the game? Blimey, it was a traumatic enough wrench leaving the Meadow, never mind the wringer we went through that afternoon. Grimsby, seemingly determined to dampen the mood, scored first to set the nerves a-jangling and we were still 1-0 down at the break. After one of the softest penalty decisions known to man (or woman), Ben Davies drilled in from the spot to settle those nerves. A point would be enough so when Kelvin Langmead rose to head home in front of us for Town's second, there was a collective release of emotions for players and fans alike – it would soon be time to get the party started.

But hold on. Seconds from the end, the visitors won a corner and in the ensuing goalmouth melee, the flailing boot of a party-pooping, balloon-bursting Grimsby player hooked the ball into the net. Deflation.

It seemed cruel that our perfect ending had been denied and I remember wondering why the opponents and their fans had to celebrate in such a wild manner, considering they were finishing 15th. Such is football. We would have probably done the same. Thankfully the painting I was soon to order, and which now hangs on my bedroom wall, doesn't depict that dampener of a denouement. Still, after that barmy barnstormer of a game, we had confirmed our place in the play-offs. All back to the Meadow in nine days' time for one last farewell.

The semi-final first leg against MK Dons really was the last hurrah at Gay Meadow and unsurprisingly turned out to be an anti-climax; the grand fanfares had already taken place, and the game had little drama and ended scoreless. After the players disappeared down the tunnel for the last time, fans were allowed on to the pitch and for a few minutes we posed for photos while remembering the special times the ground had offered up over the years. Some supporters may have taken a little piece of Gay Meadow home with them that night.

Against expectations, Town produced a strong second-leg performance which meant it was 'so long Gay Meadow, we're off to Wem-ber-lee!' Of course, it was a grand day out. I was there with my six-year-old daughter Laura, my dad, my brother, my nephew Calum and niece Lucy. It was great to all be kitted out in blue and amber clobber, to wave flags, and chat as we ambled up Wembley Way. It was amazing to see thousands of Town fans packing out one part of the new stadium with a mass of Bristol Rovers supporters at the opposite end. The attendance of 61,589 was a record for a fourth-tier game. The day got even better when Stuart Drummond glanced in a pinpoint Neil Ashton free kick within three minutes. Sadly, prolific Pirates striker Richard Walker was on top form and replied with two very well-taken goals before half-time. As Town threw everything into attack near the end, Rovers broke away and added a third. It was my first experience watching Shrewsbury at Wembley. It ended in defeat and felt painful. Over the next 11 years, this was a feeling I would need to get used to.

2007/08

Hello New Meadow

August 2007 was the dawning of 'A New Era' and that was the title of the 130-page limited edition souvenir programme, issued for the first home league game at the New Meadow, against Bradford City. Whereas the 'End of an Era' programme had pretty much been a full-on nostalgia-fest commemorating Gay Meadow, this edition pointed ahead and suggested a more corporate outlook, highlighting particular income-generating features of the new stadium such as the Legends Suite and the

Sovereign Club with images of the à la carte restaurant. It looked as though club hospitality would now be on a rather different level to the 'throwback' experience we had enjoyed with Chic Bates in the old players' lounge.

There was a lot of talk about 'New Beginnings' with informative pieces about the ticket system, the travel plan and even 'looking after the grass'. There was an interesting piece about the auction of items from Gay Meadow. It would be nice to own one of the turnstiles or the dugout. Slightly less interesting for most football fans were the 23 pages showing a month-by-month 'pictorial document of the construction of the new stadium with exclusive pictures from the build'. Another feature, entitled 'coming to terms with the change', suggested that the move would bring anxieties and it might take some time to settle. Importantly, the programme contained plenty of contributions from supporters and a section on the club's Football in the Community scheme. Town clearly had their heart in the right place, it was just time for a change, time to move upwards and onwards. Let the new era begin!

As the teams ran out that day, the pitch looked immaculate. Richard, the head groundsman, and his team had clearly done the job well. By all accounts (well, the one in the programme), using a fibre sand system gives a 'firm, fast and free-draining playing surface'.

I can also confidently state that the sward had been examined regularly for signs of fungal activity, watered, brushed, mown, groomed, fertilised and the soil tested. I'm not totally sure in what order those actions were carried out, but the results looked very impressive. Muddy encounters on boggy pitches or postponements would be less frequent going forward. Town got off to an encouraging start at their new home (attendance 6,413), a Dave Hibbert penalty after nine minutes enough to see off Stuart McCall's Bantams and earn three points. The rest of the season did not go so positively. Manager Gary Peters was replaced by Paul Simpson and the club finished 18th, firmly positioned in the 'room for improvement' category.

2008/09

Seven up, one down

By the beginning of the following season, the stadium had a new title sponsor – Prostar – but most fans tended to go with 'New Meadow'. I was sitting in the family stand with my daughter for the Gillingham game in September and based on what we saw that day, it seemed that things were definitely looking up. It wasn't just the 7-0 scoreline that suggested clear progress, but the contribution of one individual wearing the number 16 shirt that stood out. It was the first time I'd seen

Town's £170,000 record signing from Nottingham Forest, Grant Holt, and I very much liked what I saw. Powerful and skilful, Holt may not have been the best performer on the pitch that day – Ben Davies deserved that accolade – but he earned, then scored the resulting penalty, got booked and remained a constant handful for the Gills' defence all afternoon. This guy clearly had class, a level of class higher than League Two. But he'd signed for Shrewsbury and now we had the pleasure of watching this exceptional striker filling his boots. Which is exactly what Grant Holt did that season, banging in five at Wycombe in the Football League Trophy along the way and ending up with 20 league goals.

One of Holt's most important strikes was the first against Dagenham & Redbridge on the last day, which helped clinch the final play-off spot. Chris Humphrey got the other goal. The 1-0 semi-final first leg home defeat by Bury was poor but Town clawed back the deficit in the return to set up a second Wembley play-off final in two years. This time we'd be playing Gillingham, the team we'd trounced earlier in the season. This time we'd get it right, right?

Er, wrong, I'm afraid. We had headed to the familiar venue, this time taking the Chiltern Line from Warwick Parkway. It was an early morning departure, but I was surprised how many blue-and-amber-clad fans were on the train. The carriage was crowded and noisy, with plenty of drinking, chanting and banter. I'm pretty sure I spotted former Town defender Nigel Pearson looking serious and trying to keep a low profile, perhaps preparing for a punditry role.

We ambled up Wembley Way again, posing for photos. At the statue of England's 1966 World Cup-winning captain, we bumped into a former pupil who my dad had taught at Bishop's Castle County High school, who uttered the line: 'Two legends in one place: Bobby Moore and Mr Preshous!' That went down well with our group. Inside the famous stadium I was quite shocked to see so many Gillingham fans banked away opposite us. Where did they all come from?! A crowd of 53,706 was whopping but unfortunately the contingent from Shropshire would not be celebrating that day. Just as a tight match seemed to be heading into extra time, in the 90th minute Simeon Jackson took advantage of some hesitation in the Town defence to head in the winner. The Kentish hordes went wild, while we just sat there in shocked silence, devastated by this late turn of events.

Our star striker couldn't influence the outcome that day but at least Grant Holt did achieve some significant accolades that season, ending up a joint top scorer for the division, winning the League Two Player of the Year award and being named in the League Two PFA Team of the Year. He was voted Shrewsbury's Player of the Year too. We knew that Holt was one of the best players we'd ever seen in a Town shirt. In July 2009, he left for Norwich City.

2009/10
Cup of woe

In recent years, Shrewsbury themselves had been on the receiving end of some FA Cup shocks, losing at Histon in 2004 and at Blyth Spartans in 2008. I was relieved that I didn't travel to watch either of those calamities. In the programme for Town's FA Cup first round game in 2009, both captain and manager stated how pleased they were to get a home draw. Centre-back Graham Coughlan was careful not to underestimate the opposition, saying that they would be a 'tough, tough test', while boss Paul Simpson made his feelings clear, 'They are a side with a lot of energy about them and have a lot of pace so we will need to be aware of that threat.' Come on fellas – this was Staines Town from the Blue Square South! Okay, they'd surprised a few people (maybe about 17?) by beating Hayes & Yeading away in the previous round, but their other cup victories had been against Walton Casuals (weren't they a Mod revival band?) and Sittingbourne. We weren't playing Liverpool (that would be another day)!

This was a home banker, so my dad and I took our seats in block 15 expecting a smooth passage to round two. Coughlan and Simpson had been right to be cautious but had not heeded their own warnings. Staines *were* a tough test, showed energy, pace and not only threatened, but actually dealt the fatal blow with a stunning individual goal from Ali Chaaban. You couldn't begrudge the players and staff celebrating with their handful of fans at the end, but Town were out and it was embarrassing. That was a low point of a mediocre season and up there with my lowest Town low points. Simpson was axed with two games remaining that season.

2010/11

Turner returns and turns it on again

Cometh pre-season, cometh our man. After a 26-year 'break' at Aston Villa, Wolves and Hereford, Graham Turner returned to manage Shrewsbury again and made an immediate impact. Town finished in fourth place, narrowly missing out on the automatic spots by a point. I wasn't at the 1-1 home game with promotion contenders Wycombe in March, but I do know that Gareth Ainsworth's 'ghost goal' still rankles for those who were there. I like Ainsworth, love his laid-back image, the positive attitude and totally respect what he's done for the Chairboys, but Gareth, you do owe us one for that moment – maybe come and manage us someday? Irritatingly, Wycombe snaffled the third remaining slot and went up, so Town had to go again versus seventh-place finishers Torquay United. The first game away didn't go to plan but for the home leg, even though Town were 2-0 down, there was still a raucous atmosphere in the south stand of the now-named Greenhous Meadow. Fans were clearly hoping for an exciting contest and a dramatic comeback. Instead, it ended 0-0; a limp, lacklustre Friday evening. Turner's dream return to the club hadn't quite materialised. We would have to wait, but not for too long.

2011/12

Up where we belong

The chants of 'Sacked in the morning! You're getting sacked in the morning' heard on a Tuesday evening in September 2011 were not aimed at Graham Turner, but at his counterpart at the Emirates Stadium that night. In one of those rare, wondrous, odds-confounding moments, James Collins met Marvin Morgan's sumptuous cross with a powerful header and the ball flew past Łukasz Fabiański into the back of the Arsenal net. It may have only been the third round of the League Cup but the 5,000-plus Town fans didn't hold back from celebrating and then began goading the home fans and their under-pressure manager, Arsène Wenger. It was a beautiful 17 minutes leading the Gunners in their backyard and though they had not fielded their strongest 11, a mix of youth and experience eventually proved too strong for the Shrews. Kieran Gibbs headed in an equaliser before the break, then 18-year-old Alex Oxlade-Chamberlain fired in the second with Yossi Benayoun completing the turnaround. A crowd of 46,539 watched the game that night and the away team and their following left north London with their heads held high.

The players were looking good and the squad depth looked even better. Chris Neal was a safe pair of hands between the sticks. Jermaine Grandison was a gangly but skilful right-back, heading for cult status for his mazy runs and multiple step-overs (which he sometimes overdid when his gangly legs became a bit tangled up). Joe Jacobson was a reliable full-back with a sweet left peg who could deliver pinpoint corners and free kicks. These attributes were employed to even more devastating effect at his next club, Wycombe – aarrrghhh! Ian Sharps and Shane Cansdell-Sherriff combined authority and strength with some finesse at the centre of the defence. In midfield, Sean and David McAllister, Nicky Wroe, Matt Richards and Lionel Ainsworth were all good options while Collins, Morgan, Terry Gornell and Mark Wright supplied most of the goals. Keeper Ben Smith,

Reuben Hazell, James Hurst, Carl Regan, Jon Taylor and Aaron Wildig also made decent contributions that season. And there were a handful of appearances from Tom Bradshaw, Connor Goldson and Romaine Sawyers, whose days would come.

The bouquet on the 2011/12 Town vintage was steely rather than velvety but after a 1-0 loss at Plymouth on 17 March and lying in fourth position (and not wanting a repeat of the previous season's pathetic play-off capitulation), with ten matches remaining, the team tightened up and raised their game. Victories over Cheltenham, Morecambe, Macclesfield, Bradford, Rotherham and Port Vale and a draw with Aldershot meant that a win at Accrington Stanley would get the Shrews past the post to promotion.

The name of this Lancashire-based club alone is evocative for most long-term followers of football, but I had a soft spot for Stanley as at a previous encounter at the Meadow, a friendly away fan had spread the love by giving me and my daughter two Stanley pin badges. It was a nice gesture so I was more than happy to drive up from Warwickshire, put some money in their club coffers and then celebrate promotion. Well, the first part worked out. I purchased an Accrington Stanley notebook and a programme in the club shop. When the team coach arrived, I got Graham Turner's signature on the front cover, then Marvin Morgan scribbled his name on the back. I took my place on the open terraces of the Crown Ground behind the goal. It was a great turnout, and we were rewarded when Terry Gornell spun and rifled in directly in front of the Shropshire supporters. Disappointingly, on 78 minutes, Stanley's Bryan Hughes drove home and celebrated with his team-mates.

I also drove home but our celebrations were on hold, although we didn't have to wait long – the following Saturday, Town completed the job by beating Dagenham & Redbridge 1-0, James Collins again heading in the winner. There were people on the pitch. They thought it was all over. It was. Town were back in the third tier of English football for the first time in 15 years, though it was now called League One. It was the second time Turner had completed the season with an undefeated home record (the first time was 1978/79) and it was a club record points tally of 88. It could have been more. After nine games without losing, and clearly on a roll, Shrewsbury went to AFC Wimbledon on the final day of the season and lost 3-1.

2012/13

Little fish, big fish, swimming in the water

Many thought Town would drop straight back down but credit to Turner and his team, they survived, with two of the best results coming against a club playing in the third tier for the first time in nearly 50 years. Coventry City were certainly a big fish at this level, and now there would be two new Midlands derbies to look forward to on the fixture list.

As an exiled Shrew, living in Warwickshire, the Sky Blues were my nearest Football League club. I worked in the city and had friends and colleagues who were Cov fans. I was excited by the prospect and in mid-September, the first meeting that season took place at the Greenhous Meadow. Neither side had started the season promisingly; Town had one win and were in 19th place, while City were languishing second from bottom without a win. And that run continued as the home side produced a strong performance to crush the visitors from Coventry. Darren Jones headed an early goal to set the tone and Paul Parry doubled the lead on 20 minutes so by the break, the 600 or so away fans were clearly not happy bunnies and were expressing their ire via earthy terminology and rudimentary gestures, much to our amusement and pleasure. And it didn't get any better for them. In the second half, a Matt Richards penalty and Marvin Morgan strike sealed the outcome with a John Fleck consolation penalty hardly easing the pain for the away following. Well, at least they didn't have far to go. I had a similar journey to take back along the

M54 and M6 but my mood was very different. I was very tempted to wave cheerily at the Cov fans I passed on the way home but keeping two hands on the wheel was the sensible option so I contented myself with a smug smirk aimed in their general direction.

The return encounter at the cavernous Ricoh Arena was on New Year's Day 2013 in front of 15,185. Town were still in 19th place, without an away win all season and had drawn four out of their five previous games. Coventry had hit a rich vein of form and shot up to ninth position. The home fans were now confident, even cocky, wanting revenge for the September humiliation. The Salopian contingent were hoping to sneak an unlikely point and make this more than just a day out at a quality stadium of a big city club.

It was more productive and satisfying than that, as Town, playing in the red-shirted away strip, produced a solid defensive display with Morgan pouncing to stab in the decisive goal on 62 minutes. Nearly 1,500 Salopians went barmy and Shrewsbury held on to claim a valuable three points, get the first away win under their belt and perhaps most pleasingly, do the double over this former top-tier club. It was no mean achievement as Cov had players who would go on to play at higher levels, such as Cyrus Christie, John Fleck and David McGoldrick, while Gary McSheffrey had appeared in the Premier League for Birmingham City earlier in his career. The headline on the back of the *Coventry Telegraph* was 'Sorry – New Year!' Not for Shrewsbury Town and their fans, it wasn't. I enjoyed going into work after that one.

Going to a home game as an exiled Town fan requires planning, permission and time, as well as some additional financial burdens – for me, it was a two-and-a-half-hour round trip of 128 miles. There were questions to address and consider: were Shrewsbury on good form? Was the game important in some way? Would there be a good atmosphere with a decent away turnout? Would my Shropshire-based mates be going? Would Jo be okay to look after our daughters? Could I get off work a bit earlier? Could I really be arsed?

Possible answers had to be factored in and processed, which meant games had to be selected carefully. A 13th v 14th contest involving Colchester United on a Tuesday night in late October wasn't going to make the cut. If I'd been living in or nearer to Shrewsbury, that might have been a different matter. Anyway, in 2013, that match ended 1-1 so I probably made the correct decision. However, on that evening I did miss the moment that loanee Cristian López Santamaría became the first Spaniard to net for Town. A gift for the completists among the crowd of 4,364. Muy bien.

2013/14

Down, down, deeper and down

I had become a little more discerning about the matches I picked to attend and there was now some justification of labelling me a 'big game Charlie': Coventry, Wolves (home and away) and Galatasaray seemed to indicate this anyway. As mentioned earlier, I'd seen Shrewsbury play friendlies against Zambia and Tulsa Roughnecks but the pre-season fixture against the reigning Turkish champions seemed equally bizarre. And I wasn't going to miss it. The biggest name on view and biggest attraction was Didier Drogba, the former Chelsea star, and people clustered around him to get his signature, a photo or just a whiff of his aura. I managed to get another footballing giant, Dutchman Wesley Sneijder, to sign the cover of my programme. This edition showed young Town players on a training run heading up a Shropshire hill, with Connor Goldson near the front of the pack.

At the game, a small cohort of Galatasaray followers made a bit of noise and let off some flares. It was a hot July day and the team from Istanbul were just too hot for their League One hosts. Goals by Emre Çolak and Nordin Amrabat made the difference at half-time with Sneijder wrapping things up just before the end. Town fans also got a glimpse of other former Premier League players in Emmanuel Eboué, Albert Riera and Colin

Kazim-Richards but there was no doubting who the main draw was and there was excitement all around the ground when Drogba came on as a second-half substitute. One large, shirtless Chelsea fan couldn't contain himself and ran on to the pitch to show off a tattoo of Drogba inked on his back, earning a sweaty hug from the stellar striker. This individual pitch invasion didn't go down well with the locals but when keeper Joe Anyon palmed away a left-foot drive from the famous forward, there was generous applause around the Greenhous Meadow. Until the next time, Didier.

A few weeks on, Galatasaray won the Emirates Cup, beating Porto and Arsenal, with Drogba scoring twice against the Gunners in front of just under 60,000. Later that season the Turkish club went on to beat Juventus in the UEFA Champions League group stage before getting knocked out in the last 16 by the Ivorian's former club, Chelsea.

In late November 2013, just after Galatasaray played Real Madrid in the Bernabéu (and got pummelled 4-1), I was heading to the Lamex Stadium, Stevenage, for the climax of my 50th birthday celebrations. The proceedings had started on Friday when I'd spent a day at St George's Park, England's training facility near Burton-on-Trent, invited by my good friend Orhan, who had won a day out there. We enjoyed a tour of the facilities and training sessions held by staff and some of the England women's football team. At lunch, Alex Scott and Jordan Nobbs sat at our table and were down to earth, friendly hosts. 'Uncle Trev' Brooking was the guest speaker and later patiently signed autographs and posed for photos until the long queue dispersed. I had brought along my 1982 K-Tel England World Cup LP *This Time* (in gatefold sleeve) for him to sign and Brooking chuckled before saying, 'Oh yes, I remember that.' He probably also remembered that England, that time, didn't get it right and we didn't bring it up either.

Clutching a signed football and various other memorabilia, we headed to Northampton for the second event in the celebratory weekend. We rendezvoused with my brother and a few other close friends at the Premier Inn (no expense spared!) and enjoyed a sharpener or two before watching Half Man Half Biscuit at The Roadmenders. What glamour! As ever, the Biccies were in fine form. The next morning, we headed off for the *pièce de résistance* of the weekend: Stevenage versus Shrewsbury. And our Town came up trumps. Although François Zoko scored first for the home team, Adam Reach, Tom Eaves and Joe Jacobson were on the scoresheet for the Shrews, all names who would go on to play at Championship level. There weren't many away wins that season (or at home, for that matter), but down at the Lamex, the team did the business to cap a great 48 hours and complete a successful away day for a small band of Salopians plus a few 'guest' fans.

Town were still struggling though – in December I was back at the Meadow for dispiriting 1-0 losses against Walsall and Preston, two teams with boisterous away followings, which always made matters worse. After losing 3-0 to Rotherham in January, the club's sixth consecutive home defeat, Graham Turner called it a day and handed in his notice. Former player Michael Jackson took over.

In March I made the short M45/M1 journey down to Sixfields, Coventry City's temporary home in Northampton to watch a dull 0-0 affair. A handful of hardcore Coventry fans were visible on raised ground, outside the stadium loudly protesting against the serious issues affecting their club. After the previous season's double over the Sky Blues, this time it was honours even on both occasions. Later that month I met my pals at Molineux to watch the team gain a hard-earned point when we really needed three. To dispel those 'big game Charlie' accusations, I even went to the return fixture with Stevenage in April – a positive result thanks to a solitary Jon Taylor strike, which offered a smidgen of hope. In the subsequent four games, that ickle wickle trickle of hope was brutally eliminated with four defeats.

Town were relegated and joined the League Two small fry again.

2014/15

New horizons

No worries. It's always a pleasure to visit and tick off a new ground, which is what I did on the opening day of this campaign, meeting my south London-based mate and honorary Shrews fan, Orhan, at the Kingsmeadow home of AFC Wimbledon. We hung around near the main entrance before the game and looked at a pin badge seller's merchandise. I almost shrieked when I spotted a badge for Bishop's Castle Football Club on the board. How bizarre. We then stepped aside as Adebayo Akinfenwa, a recent Dons signing, headed towards the players' entrance exchanging genial banter with supporters. I wish we'd got a photo with him. What a legend. Town fans were in good voice that day and were getting behind the boss with sustained chanting of 'Micky Mellon's barmy army'. It was an exciting contest and a late equaliser from James Collins, his second, meant the spoils were shared in a 2-2 draw.

Overall, it turned out to be a very good campaign for Town and one game even threw up a collector's item of a Connor Goldson brace (2-0 v Dagenham & Redbridge). However, my forays to watch games were infrequent that season and family commitments prevented me from getting to the penultimate and decisive match at Cheltenham when Jean-Louis Akpa Akpro's winner sealed promotion. I did get over for the final-day meeting with Plymouth and though there was a celebratory mood, the occasion was slightly muted by a 2-0 home defeat. Town would be returning to the third tier of English football but were now in danger of becoming a League One/League Two yo-yo club, which can get a bit tiresome.

6
Cup distractions

OVER SIX years from 2014 to 2020, Town had some amazing cup encounters, creating distractions from the lower-league fodder of Stevenage and bloody Bury. This sequence all began in the League Cup (or Capital One Cup at that time) with a home victory over Blackpool in manager Micky Mellon's first season. An improbable away win at Premier League Leicester in the second round was the first shock and set up a home tie with Norwich City. The Canaries had just dropped down to the Championship but still had a good reputation in football circles so this would be an interesting tussle.

I drove over from Warwickshire with Kevin, an Ipswich-supporting mate, keen to give his support to Shrewsbury and see the Tractor Boys' arch-rivals get knocked out. Over 5,000 Town fans, including an

Ipswich one, went home very happy that night as James Collins again proved his worth by nodding the winner past the Norwich keeper in the second half. I'm sure somewhere around the country there was a match review of the game which ran with the headline 'Canaries knocked off their perch'. Probably the *Suffolk County Times*, if that actually existed.

Shrewsbury hadn't been this far in the competition since 1986/87. A peachy draw would be nice. And please, oh footballing gods, not MK Dons. Bingo – Chelsea at home. Again. Welcome back Didier, and hola, José! Managers Mellon and Mourinho would face each other, and both were on the cover of the *Town Talk* programme. And what a night it was. It's worth having a look at the line-ups (including the substitutes who came on) to highlight what the home side were facing:

Shrewsbury: Jayson Leutwiler, Jack Grimmer, Connor Goldson, Nathaniel Knight-Percival, Jermaine Grandison, Mickey Demetriou, Bobby Grant (Jordan Clark), Ryan Woods, Liam Lawrence (C), James Collins (Andy Mangan), Jean-Louis Akpa Akpro.

Chelsea: Petr Čech, Andreas Christensen, Gary Cahill, Kurt Zouma, Filipe Luís, Mikel John Obi (Willian), Nathan Aké, Mohamed Salah (Nemanja Matić), Oscar (Eden Hazard), Didier Drogba (C), André Schürrle.

Lordy lordy. How would Shrewsbury cope against a first 11 packed full of internationals and even a World Cup winner in Schürrle? Best not to think about who lay in wait on the bench. But Town coped admirably and the London team soon found out that they were in a contest. Late in the first half there was a worrying moment when tricky winger Mohamed Salah cut in from the right and ominously cued up to shoot on his stronger left foot. The Egyptian's shot was wildly inaccurate and flew upwards, then bounced out for a throw-in by the family stand. There were loud guffaws from the home fans at this comedy moment.

Mo, the Special One and his players did have the last laugh, though not without experiencing some nervy passages. The Premier League team took the lead early in the second half when Salah laid off a Schürrle pass to Drogba who swept the ball past Leutwiler in front of the Chelsea fans. Late in the game, Mellon made a substitution which had an almost instant impact when Andy Mangan hooked in a loose ball with his first touch on 77 minutes. Bedlam for thousands of Salopians. Unfortunately, Town didn't hold on for long and under pressure from Drogba again, Grandison headed into his own net. It was a heroic defeat before a record attendance at the stadium of 10,210. The home team got a loud ovation at the end as handshakes were exchanged. Mourinho was respectful and complimented the Town players for making it difficult for his side but commended his own players' professionalism. Well, with a squad worth over £300m, you'd expect that really, wouldn't you? Mellon expressed disappointment, which says a lot, and was clearly proud of the shift his team had put in. The most impressive performance on the night for me was by 20-year-old Ryan Woods, calmly stroking passes about, intercepting play and showing an assurance that didn't look out of place among all those multimillion-pound internationals.

The following season it was the FA Cup that provided the main thrills, with the run starting in the first round at the humble setting of The Northolme, home of Gainsborough Trinity. Town negotiated this non-league hurdle with a James Collins drive deciding the outcome. Shrewsbury had to travel in the same direction for the second round, just a little further east to Grimsby where they drew 0-0 before a very late Abu Ogogo goal in the replay put them through. The third-round draw set up a meeting with old rivals Cardiff City. The match was rescheduled to a Sunday evening which put me off travelling down to South Wales. It must have also put off a few others as the piffling crowd of 4,782 was one of the lowest ever at the Cardiff City Stadium. For Town fans, that didn't matter as Mangan, on his return to the club, settled the tie with a headed winner. As Cardiff were sitting 35 places above Shrewsbury in ninth position in the Championship, this could be classed as a surprise result, and was gratefully received, thank you very much.

For the first time on that cup run, Mickey Mellon's team were then rewarded with a home game in the fourth round, drawing Sheffield Wednesday, who were just outside the play-off berths in the Championship. In contrast, Town were just above the relegation zone in League One. This sounded tempting and I wasn't going to miss it. That season, the *Town Talk* programme had taken on the appearance of a glossy men's fashion brochure with players shown in casual shots on the cover and their detailed profiles within. For example, for the Chesterfield game (lost 2-1), there was Jean-Louis Akpa Akpro, leaning on a barrier next to the River Severn with the English Bridge, Wakeman School and Abbey Foregate Chapel as a backdrop. All familiar sights if you'd been heading to Gay Meadow pre-2007. Jean-Louis was kitted out in a grey hoody and jeans, gazing enigmatically into the middle distance. Cool.

For Walsall (lost 3-1), it was a head-and-shoulders shot of Larnell Cole on the cover, sporting a dark green sweatshirt, a serious look and eyes aimed away from the camera. His expression must have changed a bit on the night as he grabbed Town's only goal. For the Boxing Day game against Fleetwood (drew 1-1), Anthony Gerrard, cousin of Steven, was shown wearing a club training top. He was laughing wholeheartedly, perhaps to provide some festive cheer and with our team mired near the drop-zone, goodness me, we needed some.

To be fair, the programmes were packed full of great content, including embedded facsimiles of old programmes, a feature I loved, but the cover did look like an advert for menswear or male grooming. For the Sheffield Wednesday cup game, it was 22-year-old Jack Grimmer, male model, I mean, Scottish full-back on loan from Fulham. Standing in front of some reddish-brown vegetation, Jack was wearing a trendy-looking khaki jacket and a winning smile. In the feature there were more photos of Grimmer next to a field of tall yellow plants clad in the same gear and one full-length picture in the blue and amber kit. The programme even contained a massive colour poster of our Jack (with a black and white portrait of Ian Atkins on the back). It would turn out to be quite a day for this young man.

Carlos Carvalhal's Owls took control in the first half when a Lewis McGugan free kick sailed past everyone into the corner of the net to put the visitors one up at half-time. Akpa Akpro headed in an equaliser after a swift breakaway and cross from Andy Mangan. McGugan fired in his second with another long-distance shot to put Wednesday back in the lead but it wasn't over and Town were about to launch a famous comeback. They left it late though. On 87 minutes, Akpa Akpro was clumsily tripped and though the Frenchman's resulting spot kick was parried by the keeper, substitute Sean Whalley tucked in the rebound. A replay at Hillsborough. That'll do nicely. But no, it wasn't to be. Better than that. Deep into injury time, another substitute, Scott Vernon, carried the ball down the left wing and manoeuvred to cross, while full-back Grimmer motored down the middle of the park with wanton abandonment, and with impeccable timing, arrived to nod home. He ran towards the ecstatic Town fans in the South Stand, was embraced, and promptly fell over before a mighty bundle ensued. It was a dramatic ending to a humdinger of a game. Town were in the hat for the fifth round of the FA Cup for the first time in 25 years. It had been a fantastic day for the whole club, the fans and one young Scotsman in particular. The *Sunday Times* match report led with the headline 'Shrewsbury strike late to make life grim and Grimmer for Wednesday'. Nice. In post-match interviews, Jack's winning smile was on show again.

Mark Lawrenson and Ruud Gullit were the pundits responsible for setting up a history-making tie by pitting two teams together who had never played each other competitively: Shrewsbury Town at home to Manchester United. Mad scenes in Shropshire households, pubs and at one home in Kenilworth, Warwickshire. This was a great opportunity for the Shrews to pull off a massive shock and although Sir Alex Ferguson had left and United certainly weren't in their pomp, they were still a top-end Premier League football club and had won the FA Cup 11 times. But they'd never won the Welsh Cup, which the home team had won on six occasions, as a cheeky columnist stated in the programme.

On this occasion, Micky Mellon was hoping to outwit his counterpart, Dutch supremo Louis van Gaal. It was very much a potential banana skin for United, who were on a poor run of form, with speculation swirling around that José Mourinho was soon to get a phone call about managing the Old Trafford club. After the customary online ticketing bunfight, we secured seats in block 17 on that February evening in front of the TV cameras, anticipating either a famous victory or glorious defeat. We got neither. Although Town didn't play that badly, the threat offered was minimal, the gap in class starkly evident. Chris Smalling and Juan Mata scored before the break, and Jesse Lingard pulled the trigger for the third to put United into the next round. It was a chastening, disappointing evening, nothing like some of the blood, mud and thunder cup ties we'd witnessed in the past.

On the cover of the programme, Dominic Smith appeared, looking pensive and smartly attired in a navy blue, zipped jacket. During the game, Dominic's expression probably remained pensive as he remained on the subs' bench. Oh well, at least, we could say, we'd been knocked out by the eventual cup winners as Manchester United went on to beat Crystal Palace in the 2016 final, with goals from Mata and Lingard again. It was their 12th triumph in the competition. Six Welsh Cup titles though. Just saying.

7

The later years

BACK IN the league, there was a narrow escape in 2015/16 with Town finishing just above the relegation places. The 2016/17 season started badly and after ten games, Mickey Mellon was on his bike. In October a new manager was installed, performances improved and Shrewsbury did enough to finish in 18th, two points above the trapdoor to League Two. There were no cup distractions that season as the club were knocked out in the early rounds.

2017/18

Oh so near and yet oh so far

To almost everybody's surprise and wonderment, this campaign brought a remarkable turnaround in league form and fortunes, with some uplifting then disheartening cup exploits thrown in for good measure.

For a while, it even looked like we might be getting a modern-day version of 1978/79. Let's hear it for the almost legendary Paul Hurst season. It really was one hell of a ride.

Hurst, the former Grimsby Town manager, and his trusty assistant Chris Doig had been appointed the previous autumn and had steered Town to safety. But it had been slim pickings for the supporters with no obvious signs of what lay ahead. Pre-season friendlies aren't always a reliable gauge either but home wins over Aston Villa, Wolves and Cardiff caused a few raised eyebrows. Away defeats to Brackley Town and AFC Telford lowered them again. On the opening day, a very late winner from Lenell John-Lewis ('The Shop') gave Town the perfect start and another six points were added by beating AFC Wimbledon and Rochdale.

Encouraged by and curious about these promising signs, I headed down the M40, dropped off my daughters at one of Oxford's park and ride points so they could go shopping in the city, and headed along the A34 to visit the Kassam Stadium for the first time. Town didn't win the game and didn't set a new club record of four consecutive victories at the start of a season, but I kid you not, that match was a revelation. And it wasn't just because three new Shrewsbury players I was witnessing for the first time stood out, although they did have a significant influence that day, and for the rest of the campaign. On loan from Norwich, 19-year-old Ben Godfrey made a highly effective debut in midfield and the exquisite skills of Jon Nolan, a recent signing from Chesterfield, shone brightly too. Overall though, it was the team performance that made the biggest impression that afternoon. All over the pitch, players in that bright orange away strip were working tirelessly, seemed to be in control and most pleasingly, were playing some remarkable football. It really was a joy to behold. The away fans in the North Stand were showing their appreciation and we all thought Carlton Morris had scored but it was adjudged that the ball had not crossed the goal line. It seemed like a harsh decision and to compound the situation, Oxford took the lead with 15 minutes to go.

Hurst's team were not going to lose that day, though. No way. And sure enough, one of the late substitutes, Stefan Payne, prodded in the equaliser. Even though the game ended 1-1, it had been one of the most memorable, pulsating Shrewsbury Town displays I had ever seen. After the final whistle, the Town players came over to salute their loyal following, with the young Manchester United loanee keeper Dean Henderson (the third new player I was watching for the first time) showing particular enthusiasm and then giving his cap to a young supporter. I turned to the bloke next to me and said, 'I think we're going to be all right this season,' and headed back to the car park, positively buzzing. My girls had enjoyed themselves too so all was good with the world.

As it transpired, the start of the campaign was better than 'all right'. Shrewsbury rose majestically to the top of League One and remained undefeated until late October, when they lost at Peterborough. These were terrific times for STFC supporters who couldn't really believe what was happening. During that period there were feisty away draws at Walsall and late, late wins at Doncaster, but it was the home form that was exemplary. Against Bristol Rovers, Town were four up after 41 minutes and at half-time I had never experienced such a positive, celebratory mood in the gents'. It was surreal: even the old whingers weren't whinging – they were virtually hopping with delight, gleefully enjoying the moment. That game ended 4-0 and everything was fine. By the end of 2017, Wigan were topping the table, but Town were keeping pace just behind, five points ahead of the other 'big' team in the league, Blackburn Rovers. Another element that contributed to the ride that campaign were Ollie and Glyn's regular *Salopcast* podcasts: enthusiastic, often candid, but genuine from-the-Salopian heart episodes which perfectly captured the exuberant highs, the warts and all the other stuff, whether it was injury-time winners on the road, moments of individual brilliance, exemplary team performances, stalwart rearguard action, top-of-the-table tension or the disappointing end-of-season slump, as they dissected all the scenes in the high drama being enacted before our eyes.

The team had also cruised through to the third round of the FA Cup where yet another tasty-looking draw beckoned: West Ham at home. Not only was David Moyes returning to Shropshire, but Joe Hart was recalled by the Hammers and made captain for the day, against his hometown club. He received a good reception from the Salopian fans and was one of the visitors' best players (which isn't saying much really as their performance was poor), making some important saves, particularly a point-blank block to deny a certain goal from Mat Sadler. After the game, Hurst said his team were 'a little bit deflated almost' and there was definitely a sense of a missed giant-killing opportunity. I couldn't get to the replay but listened to the live commentary as Town held on deep into extra time before being knocked out. If I'm perfectly honest, I was secretly relieved that I hadn't missed a famous victory at the London Stadium or would be facing a tiring journey back home in the early hours. At least it had been an income-generator for the club and now, even though it was a cliché, we *really* could concentrate on the league.

Inevitably, there had been a slight drop-off in the early season form, especially at home, and Blackburn had taken over at the top by late February. Yet the away results were still impressive so that month, I met a friend in London, we quaffed a couple of pints of London Pride and, together with a large, noisy contingent from Shropshire, experienced a fruitful away day at The Valley with a 2-0 win over Charlton. Just over two weeks later, Town were still in second place in the table, but Wigan had games in hand so winning at Northampton was vital. It was a frustrating evening at the Sixfields Stadium, and just as the 1-1 draw at Oxford had oozed positive vibes, this 1-1 felt like a complete downer. Abu Ogogo was sent off along with one of their players for some sort of wrestling antics and though Nolan equalised soon after that incident, chances were squandered, and the score remained level. It felt like a pivotal point in the season, but not in a good way.

There were other cup distractions that season, and in retrospect, progress in a lesser-known competition might have been more detrimental on the promotion challenge. The Football League Trophy (now sponsored by Checkatrade) was not widely loved but Town had negotiated a safe passage to the semi-final, overcoming Coventry City, West Brom's under-21s and Blackpool en route. Thankfully they'd avoided the highly rated Chelsea under-10 junior team who were in a different group. But not really. Town would now play Yeovil and it seemed remiss to pass up a chance to get back to Wembley again when so close. A second-half Carlton Morris goal duly lined up another trip to the national stadium. By the time of the final, Wigan had powered into second place in League One so the mood was a little less buoyant, but getting a trophy under the belt against League Two Lincoln would be a fillip for the final promotion push. I'm sure there were plenty of Checkatrade dissenters who didn't make the journey south, but Town were favourites and it would be great to get that Wembley monkey off our back (played three, lost three). The game didn't start well when burly Imps henchman striker Matt Rhead poleaxed Dean Henderson. A few minutes later, our man between the sticks, possibly still dazed, unsuccessfully attempted to clear a corner and Danny Cowley's team went 1-0 up. And that's how it ended. On a damp day, it had been a damp squib and the Wembley hoodoo remained.

For the last six league games of the season, it wasn't that the wheels had come off exactly, more that the team seemed to be running out of steam after all their exertions (including additional cup game time) and so many high-level, energy-draining performances. There was only one victory in that time while Wigan and Blackburn drove on to automatic promotion, leaving Town in their wake with many of us wondering if the season would just sputter out into an empty void of nothingness (yes, I know that's tautological, but you get the point, it all seemed rather bleak). Ten minutes from the end of the play-off semi-final first leg back at The Valley, Jon Nolan re-ignited the fire as his blistering half-volley rocketed into the top-right corner of the Charlton net. It was a thing of beauty and all the hope and joy returned in an instant. In the return leg, again it was Carlton Morris who netted to confirm another Wembley outing.

This time, it had to be written in the stars that Shrewsbury would triumph and be on their way back to the second tier. Heck, Town had finished eight points above Rotherham so surely deserved to be promoted after such a good reason, right? Paul Hurst would be facing his former club and had actually played for the Millers when they had beaten Town in the 1996 Football League Trophy Final. I wasn't really sure if that was a good omen or not. Basically, doubts were creeping in again.

Two of my Shropshire-based Town fan mates had cited half-term family holiday commitments and would not be coming to the game but would be heading to the Welsh coast. Bottlers. The match attendance of

26,218 suggested that many others were away or indeed, bottling it – it was a record low crowd for a third-tier play-off final. Still, a mate from Leamington and my friends in the south were up for it and would be Town fans for a day. Again.

The sun was shining – this was more like Wembley weather and perked everyone up, a far cry from the rainy-day misery we'd experienced at the same venue a few weeks previously. After nine minutes, a punch in the gut. Penalty to Rotherham. But there was Hendo the Hero, yards off his line to save the penalty and possibly the season. Maybe it *was* going to be our day? After 32 minutes, a body blow – Richard Wood charged into a gaping hole in the Town defence to head the opening goal. Despondency in the ranks. In the second half, there was a spirited fightback and a brilliant set-piece routine allowed Alex Rodman (an ex-Leamington FC player, as my mate gleefully pointed out) to steer the ball home. That cheered us all up.

The game went into extra time; we moved to seats away from the glare of the sun and watched in near silence as Wood stole in for his second. This time the Town players looked spent, and we sensed that the pesky Wembley curse had struck again. The running total was now five visits and five defeats. It was very hard to take after such an amazing campaign but when the match ended, we showed our appreciation to the manager and players for their efforts while I tried really hard not to think about being on the beach at Aberdovey, enjoying the late afternoon sun. Three days later, Paul Hurst moved on to manage Ipswich Town, with Nolan and Toto Nsiala following him later that summer. The loans of Ben Godfrey, Dean Henderson and Carlton Morris ended, and they returned to their parent clubs. The dream team had been dismantled and who knew when Town would find themselves in such a position again.

2018/19

Predictably, there was a slump in this campaign with former Macclesfield Town manager John Askey out of a job by November and replaced by Sam Ricketts. The most memorable games were again in the FA Cup. In the third round, the chance to progress against Stoke City seemed to have slipped by when 37-year-old substitute Peter Crouch popped up at the back post to draw the Championship club level. All back to the Potteries for the replay. A fourth-round home tie with Wolves was the appetising bait. After the home side's Tyrese Campbell scored two well-taken goals before half-time at the Bet365 Stadium, it looked like all bets were off. But something strange and wonderful occurred on that chilly February night in Stoke. Maybe Ricketts delivered a motivating team talk in the dressing room. Maybe he dished out the hairdryer treatment. Or maybe it was the archetypal game of two halves and Town simply played brilliantly in the second 45 and Stoke were simply shit.

Anyway, it started with a scorcher, James Bolton smashing in a reply that the Town fans watched in delight as the ball arrowed into the top corner. We didn't seriously believe the comeback was possible until Josh Laurent advanced purposefully into the box and was clumsily tripped for a penalty. The Shrews fans gave a mighty roar when Fejiri Okenabirhie cooly placed the spot kick beyond the keeper. Game on! Now everyone was on their feet – let's go for the jugular and put this poor Stoke side out of their misery (and out of the cup) and make their already disgruntled fans even more disgruntled.

We didn't have to wait long as some neat right-wing trickery gave Greg Docherty the chance to stroke a low cross across the six-yard box. From our vantage point behind the goal, we all had a stunning view of this passage of play and it almost seemed like slow motion: the pass was perfectly calibrated to elude the defenders but out of the corner of our eyes we knew that a Town player was steaming in at the far stick. And sure enough, this extraordinary moment came to pass, as Laurent timed his run and arrival immaculately to side-foot home past the helpless keeper. Mayhem in the away end. The team had performed a remarkable turnaround and the fans there that night felt they had played their part in helping suck the ball into the opposition net just below our section. Outside the ground, as we were ushered towards our cars, a few coppers even congratulated us. Maybe they were Port Vale fans. We'd witnessed a cracking comeback and couldn't wait to welcome some old cup foes back to the Meadow.

This was going to be one to savour. Picture the scene: FA Cup fourth round, a Saturday afternoon 3pm kick-off. In the blue and amber corner, a team at the lower end of League One; in the black and gold corner, a famous football club, recently back in the Premier League, and faring well in eigth place. It was just over 30 miles from Shrewsbury to Wolverhampton, along the M54, and an intense local rivalry still existed. To add a little more spice to the mix, manager Ricketts used to play for Wolves too. Oh yes, and it was 40 years since that classic quarter-final encounter back in 1979. Wouldn't it be brilliant if Town could get one over their Black Country opponents?

The matchday occasion felt like a throwback too. While waiting to meet my mates, I inveigled my way beyond security to a position close to the players' entrance as the Wolves squad disembarked from their flashy coach and made for the stadium interior. It took some self-restraint to stop myself going the full 15-year-old and asking for autographs, but I did get some good close-up snaps of Nuno Espírito Santo and his team. There's no denying – it was quite a thrill. Tickets had been hard to get, and we'd grabbed three together close to the pitch. What we hadn't quite grasped, until we took our seats, was that not only were we very close to the field of play (with the two rows at the front not being used), but we were also a coin's throw from the rowdy away hordes to our left, with an even more pumped-up block 19 Salopian mob salivating behind us. Here we were, three 50-something chaps, sitting on the front line, hoping that nothing was going to kick off (apart a football match, that is). We giggled nervously about being in the first line of defence and decided it would probably be wise for us not to goad or to gesticulate obscenely at the angry citizens of Wolverhampton trying to grab our attention.

The game started and was a very pleasant distraction until the later stages when events off the field became the centre of attention. Early in the second half, Greg Docherty blasted a powerful angled shot past Wolves keeper Ruddy to light the touch paper. On 71 minutes, Oliver Norburn prepared to take a corner, consulted a piece of paper and lofted the ball on to Luke Waterfall's head to put Town two up with 15 minutes to go, and that's when trouble on the terraces ignited. The gloves were off and the epicentre of the skirmishing was our corner as the rival fans rushed to confront each other, with police and stewards desperately trying to keep them apart to prevent a full-scale riot. Well, I told you it felt like a throwback.

Perhaps this had an effect on the Town players too, as a few minutes later, substitute Raúl Jiménez was the only one to react to a low cross and pulled a goal back for the visitors. Now, most people's attention was back on the game. When the referee signalled six minutes of added time there were groans of dismay from the home crowd, and sure enough Adama Traoré beetled down the right flank, and floated the ball over for Matt Doherty to head Wolves level. The Wolves players looked relieved while their fans celebrated as if they'd won the cup. For Town, it was simply heartbreak and desolation. We tried not to look at the supporters to our left but knew they were leaping about in wild abandon, as we would have done if we'd held on and pulled off another famous giant-killing. At least we had a chance to fight again. Second thoughts, don't mention fighting. Replay Tuesday week at Molineux.

Strangely, at Wolves we found ourselves seated on the periphery of the Shropshire contingent again, closest to the home crowd in the lower tier of the Steve Bull Stand. Mercifully, the atmosphere wasn't quite as hostile but there were still plenty of unseemly exchanges between the rival fans. Most Town supporters felt that the chance to progress in the cup had been spurned by conceding in stoppage time in the first game and weren't that surprised when Doherty scored after two minutes. This could be a long, uncomfortable night, we thought. But credit to the team, they were not discouraged, and James Bolton had the audacity to nod in a leveller from a corner. It was still backs to the wall, all hands to the pump, defensive duties for most of the half but then improbably, a hopeful Josh Laurent shot squirmed through Ruddy's hands, embarrassing the keeper and causing the unsympathetic away contingent to bellow their approval. We were 2-1 up at Molineux! It was such an unlikely turn of events that some fans got carried away in their excitement – sitting immediately in front of us, an acquaintance from our part of South Shropshire couldn't contain himself and started launching a series of verbals: 'We've rumbled 'em Town', 'Get your tickets for Bristol City' and 'Let's get three or four, Town'. He also offered a terse summation of future Ivory Coast defender Willy Boly's qualities, 'He's big and awkward.'

It was a wonderful ten minutes or so (and amusing too), but cruelly, late into first-half injury time, that man

Doherty popped up again in the box to equalise. On 62 minutes it was all over when Ivan Cavaleiro jinked through the defence to prod home the winner. One Town fan's loud riposte to the predictable chanting from the Wolves fans was aimed at those seated nearest in the Sir Jack Hayward Stand, 'I'd rather shag a sheep, than a yam-yam.' 'Speak for yourself,' I muttered to my mate. We'd ruffled, rather than rumbled them; we'd scored four goals over two games against a good Premier League side but we wouldn't be going to Ashton Gate just yet. In the final game of that season, a 0-0 result condemned another Black Country club, Walsall, to the fourth tier. Cue the not so delicate sound of gloatage from the block 19 corner.

2019/20

It was hoped that Ricketts had now bedded in as manager and a full pre-season of preparation would enable the team to improve on the previous 18th-place finish. Although the former Wrexham boss had his share of non-believers and doubters, there were many others ready to give him the benefit and to trust his judgement. As ever at the opening-day match, there was hope in the hearts of the fans, but Portsmouth would be a stern test. A 30-yard left-foot blaster from Wolves loanee Ryan Giles increased the optimism by getting the club off to a winning start – who could tell what this season might bring? For the first half of the campaign, there were more ups than downs. We witnessed two seven-goal thrillers at the Meadow – an exciting 4-3 win over Southend in September, while in November, Bristol Rovers won by the same scoreline, with ex-Town player Abu Obogo scoring a very late clincher. We took confidence in solid home successes against probable promotion contenders Sunderland (1-0), Peterborough (1-0) and Coventry (2-1). Winning at Blackpool on the Saturday before Christmas gave Town fans that lovely, timely festive boost. The club were nicely placed in 11th, ready to launch their assault on the play-off berths. And it set up the next fixture, on 26 December, perfectly.

Ah yes, the Boxing Day home game; always one of the key dates that you look out for when the fixtures are first released; 26 December 1978: Watford away – dammit! 26 December 1995: Bristol Rovers at home – get in! 26 December 2019: Rotherham at home – praise be! Over the years, I have always tried to get to the match on that day, even if the film version of *The Great Escape* is on the telly. On such days, the Boxing Day match routine usually starts with a dose of paracetamol, toast, coffee, a quick look at presents and a credit-gaining activity such as entertaining the kids or walking the dog (not a euphemism). This is shortly followed by the ceremonial hacking of the turkey remains before adding bits of cold sausage, stuffing, roasters, sprouts, basically as many trimmings I can cram into two doorstep sandwiches, and not forgetting some English mustard to give it all some oomph. Pop a few Quality Street or Roses chocolates from the large circular tin into coat pockets and way to go!

It's a 75-minute drive each way from my home in the West Midlands, but the Boxing Day fixture always creates that extra buzz of anticipation. I would meet up with friends in The Bell or The Brooklands for a pint of local bitter (for me anyway, usually a few more for my Shropshire-based mates) and some festive-flavoured bants before wandering down to the ground in high spirits. These were invariably cold occasions but there was usually a warming yuletide revelry in the air before kick-off and a bigger attendance than normal. A handful of token red and white Santa hats can often be spotted among the crowd (usually a few more in the away end – perhaps the visitors feel they have to make a bit more effort on their outing), even the odd white-beard attachment too, worn by supporters keen to extend the Christmas period as long as possible, or just a bit pissed up after too many Wem Ales. If we were lucky, the match would be a feisty affair with a positive result; a less fortunate outcome or bore draw would mean a long, lonely journey back to

Warwickshire and the prospect of yet more turkey. Oh, how we love our Boxing Day football rituals.

We should have known that it would be ruddy Rotherham who would ruin any hopes of promotion. Those meddling Millers had knocked Town out of the 1961 League Cup semi-final, triumphed in the 1996 Football League Trophy Final, and beaten us in the play-offs in 2018. It was 1-1 until deep into stoppage time when Michael Smith rose to head firmly into the net. The South Yorkshire travelling army went bananas and we watched as the play-off ship sailed off from the harbour into the distance not to be seen again that season. It was a disconsolate drive home that Boxing Day but at least *Strictly* would probably be over by the time I got home, and Town were still in the FA Cup.

Bradford and Mansfield had been the victims in the opening two rounds and though losing to Wolves in the previous season's competition had deprived us all of a trip to Ashton Gate then, this time the third round draw paired Town with Bristol City on their turf. A simple twist of fate perhaps, and oddly enough instead of travelling down to the West Country for the early kick-off, that day I was visiting a gallery dedicated to George Eliot at Nuneaton Museum. George wasn't a famous Coventry City left-back. No, she wasn't; George was a celebrated 19th-century female writer who had used those words about fate as a subtitle for her novel *Silas Marner*.

Anyway, while admiring George's writing desk and trying to imagine her penning a classic work, I was also trying to follow the game on my phone. And being hopeless at multi-tasking, one activity was taking precedence. So when City took the lead I couldn't help emitting a low-pitch groan, which provoked some disapproving looks from other visitors perusing the Victorian ephemera and a withering look from my wife Jo. After that I attempted to show more interest in the artefacts and we moved swiftly through the other rooms, learning in the local history section that Larry Grayson is 'Nuneaton's favourite son'. Sitting down for coffee and cake in the café, I shared the good news that Sean Goss had equalised. By the time we got back to the railway station, the game was over. A replay at the Meadow – we were still in the FA Cup hat. Never mind *The Mill on the Floss* and *Middlemarch* (but thanks George, all the same), what would fate hold in store for Shrewsbury Town in the fourth-round draw?

Monday evening, 6 January 2020, just after 7pm. Eyes glued to the box as Mark Chapman comperes the FA Cup fourth-round draw live on the BBC. Tonight, it's Alex Scott picking the home teams and David O'Leary plucking out their opponents. The draw commences, our team isn't mentioned, the tension builds and a couple of minutes later there are only four black balls left, with the teams and numbers highlighted helpfully on the screen: Liverpool (12), Bristol C/Shrewsbury (13), Barnsley (17) and Portsmouth (27). Now every Town fan is beginning to wonder, hope, pray and please, if there is a god, please, not Pompey away.

Scott lowers her left arm into the bowl, pulls out a ball, holds it aloft, says, 'Number 27', and gives a big smile. 'Portsmouth,' intones Chapman, 'last won the cup in 2008, of course.' 'We don't frickin' care Chappers, just pick out bloody Barnsley next!' O'Leary uses his right arm, the balls swirl around a bit, his hand grabs a ball, he presents it to the camera and reads, 'Number 17.' Before Chapman can even say 'Barnsley' we all know that fate, destiny, the luck of the draw, whatever you want to call it, thank you lord, has granted us the chance to play Liverpool. Scott does the honours again, gives an even bigger smile after lifting out the number 13 ball and even O'Leary's face breaks into a wry grin as Chappers announces, 'Bristol City or Shrewsbury at home to the Premier League leaders Liverpool.' Town fans in Shropshire, in Warwickshire, dotted around the country, all over the world are not just smiling at this point, we are going bats, bouncing off the walls, hugging, high-fiving and screeching, then calling and messaging our Salopian compadres to share the breaking news. We just have to win that replay.

Until the 89th minute, the return game looked to be edging into extra time, when Aaron Pierre unleashed a tremendous low-level drive which arrowed into the bottom corner of the Bristol City net. The players celebrated in a huge bundle with other staff over by the tunnel, the supporters rejoiced, and the commentator exclaimed excitedly, 'And mighty Liverpool are coming to the Montgomery Waters Meadow,' which sounded great but was not a line that readily trips off the tongue.

As ever, for us non-season ticket holders but fans with supporter numbers, there was the anxious wait for ticketing information and the staggered 'window' system, based on the number of games you had attended and points accrued. This became slightly more complicated if your mates had been to more or fewer matches. Anyway, Griff, Ged and I secured three seats together in block 17, while my brother would be positioned a few rows in front of us. Steven didn't follow Town as much these days, being based in Hertfordshire and committed to the Leeds United cause, but he didn't want to miss this one, so he blagged the supporter number of our dad, who couldn't be there. The game would be played on a Sunday at 5pm and yet again, the BBC cameras and a starry punditry team would be pitching up, hoping for an upset.

On the day, as Shrewsbury prepared to take on the European and world champions you could feel the excitement in the air. When the Liverpool team coach pulled up outside the stadium next to the club shop, it was surrounded by fans. Smaller kids, kitted out in blue and amber or red (or all three colours, clutching half-half scarves), were hoisted on shoulders to peer through the darkened windows in the hope of getting a glimpse of some real-life footballing superstars. And it wasn't just the youngsters who were caught up in the moment. 'It's The Beatles!' someone shouted. It certainly wasn't Rochdale. In the fan zone, full of bonhomie, we mingled with some Scousers (well, they certainly had the accent) and posed for photos together. This was a massive occasion for the club, felt like a final, our final, so why not make the most of it?

Earlier in the day, Manchester United had gone to Tranmere and battered them 6-0 while City had overwhelmed Fulham. We knew perfectly well what could happen. The Reds did field a young team but in one of the all-time classic Meadow encounters, Town nearly produced the greatest shock of all. Even if it didn't quite come off, it could certainly go down as one of the greatest, most unexpected comebacks. Eighteen-year-old Curtis Jones slid in the opener for Liverpool, but this didn't deter the home side who set up two glorious chances for Merseyside-born Shaun Whalley to equalise. Put clear through on both occasions, the first was blocked by Adrián's outstretched leg, the other screwed agonisingly wide after a clever assist from Everton fan Callum Lang. Very early in the second half, as my mate Griff ambled up the steps, smiling and carrying a tray of coffees, we watched in horror to the scene which unfurled behind him. An innocuous-looking cross drifted towards the far post where Donald Love neatly guided the ball into his own, our own, net. It really was a shocker. There was stunned silence before a couple of thousand similarly amazed, but rather more delighted away supporters, started their low-key celebrations. Poor Donald Love. Poor Griff, oblivious to this disastrous development, looking pleased to have got back to us with minimal spillage and ready for Town's second-half assault, experienced the same bemused, disappointed emotions, but moments later than the rest of us. At least he hadn't witnessed this X-rated own goal clanger live. Oh my eyes. Up in the commentary box, we knew that Joe Hart, one of our own, would be suffering with us. Even Lineker, Shearer and Wrighty would probably be making sympathetic noises after this setback, but were no doubt now expecting another trouncing.

But on this day, a day of days for Shrewsbury Town Football Club, the team played with vigour and no little skill, and supported by a passionate home crowd, stuck to their task with dogged determination. Everyone wanted a response and after an inspired change by manager Sam Ricketts on 60 minutes, we got it. Substitute Jason Cummings had only been on the pitch for a few minutes when he played a perfect through ball for Josh Laurent, who was making yet another driving run forward which was curtailed abruptly by a Larouci trip. Penalty! Up stepped Cummings to calmly stroke the ball home as Adrián dived the other way. Back in the game so let's go for it seemed to be the willing cry from the terraces.

Divock Origi, scorer of the decisive goal in the 2019 Champions League Final, had a powerful shot well saved by Max O'Leary. The game was now a fully fledged proper cup clash and on 65 minutes it was elevated to classic status. Cummings suddenly nipped past Lovren and into the box before slotting the ball past the keeper again. The Scottish striker ran off towards the corner flag this time, thumping the badge, hotly pursued by his team-mates. The stands on three sides of the Montgomery Waters Meadow erupted. Apparently, Joe Hart went mad in the commentary box. Jürgen Klopp was mad too, but it was a different kind of mad. His late substitutions weren't particularly inspired, just desperate throws of the dice to avoid a replay and another game on the Reds' congested fixture list. So on came Alex

Oxlade-Chamberlain, Mohamed Salah and Roberto Firmino. Oo 'eck. Firmino did set up a fine chance for Salah to win the game, but his header was off target. I looked left at Griff and Ged, who were both speechless and grinning inanely. This was Town's day. Chants of 'Salop, Salop' rang out. We weren't going to win the match (although we could have!), we weren't going to Wembley, but we would be going to Anfield. At the final whistle, supporters spilled on to the pitch, mobbed all the players, particularly King Cummings, the hero, then congregated under the commentary box. Hart applauded while Lineker lifted the FA Cup towards the jubilant home fans, provoking another loud roar. It was some occasion and took me back to the glory days of the late 1970s. The spirit of 1979 was alive and kicking.

The replay wasn't so good. The highlights were walking across Stanley Park towards Anfield, the pre-match gathering in the Albert pub, outside the ground, meeting some of Shaun Whalley's family and 8,000 Town fans roaring the team on to the pitch. On the downside, we were herded into a corner of the stadium with terrible views of the pitch. Klopp wasn't there and neither were most of his senior players, who were taking a mid-season break in the sun. Liverpool were fielding their youngest ever line-up and were playing quite well but when Whalley headed in, it was joy unconfined in the Anfield Road Stand. Until VAR struck, that is. Scott Golbourne was adjudged to have been offside. Gutted.

It got worse. As in the first game, a hopeful cross sailed into the Shrewsbury box and this time Ro-Shaun Williams mistimed his header and diverted the ball past the stranded O'Leary. It was another nightmarish, self-inflicted wound. Again, Cummings was brought off the bench late in the day, but this time, he wasn't able to perform miracles and there was no way back. This visit to Anfield was turning out to be worse than the 1978 school minibus trip to watch the second leg of the European Super Cup against Anderlecht. Not only was it very cold that December night on the Kop but the fog was so heavy you couldn't see what was happening on the pitch, with home fans chanting 'Oggy, Oggy tell us who scored' at keeper (and future Town player) Steve Ogrizovic. Apparently, Liverpool won 2-1.

On the February evening in 2020, I would have preferred not to have seen some of the action taking place before my eyes. The Liverpool youngsters triumphed and we walked glumly back to our cars, knowing that it would be a long drive home. And barring some kind of super slump in form, in terms of having much to play for, that was probably going to be the end of the season too. Little did we know that the season would end somewhat sooner than expected.

After the cup exit, there was a slight dip in form before wins over Doncaster and Bristol Rovers steadied the ship. Our next outing following the Town would be Coventry City away on Saturday, 14 March at St Andrew's, Birmingham. After that it would be beers, curry and Bruce Foxton's band From the Jam at The Assembly, Leamington. Then all back to mine in Kenilworth. It would be an old-school away day, with three old school friends. I couldn't wait. Turns out I had to wait. We all had to wait. All football fixtures were cancelled on 13 March 2020 due to the global Covid-19 pandemic.

It was 17 months before fans were allowed to return to stadia en masse but on Saturday, 7 August 2021, I was back at the Montgomery Waters Meadow. It was the opening day of the season, a 3pm kick-off against Burton Albion. I parked up in my usual spot, wandered through the retail park to the narrow lane to the ground and got an immediate boost from seeing 'STFC' painted in blue on the bridge under the railway. How good did it feel to be back?

Two years ago, we'd basked in the sun on the grassy verge ready for the Portsmouth opener, sipping our pints next to the fan zone as a local band churned out covers of The Jam and The Smiths. This time it was raining and the queue for the fan zone bar wasn't going anywhere fast. Undeterred, we took the alternative option, and entered the ground knowing that the Woods folks would deliver the goods with a minimum of fuss. As we approached the table holding the kegs, the bloke in front ordered eight pints of Shropshire Lad. Great. After a short delay and a few minutes of frantic pulling, we were able to enjoy our refreshments and take in the familiar sights and smells of the Meadow concourse.

The programme had been revamped as well as the team and at 3pm, the referee blew his whistle and normal service was resumed. By normal service, I mean wayward passes, hoofs towards row Z (and one stunning catch from a punter), time wasting, injury feigning, missed chances, mistimed tackles, dodgy decisions – after one particularly dubious one, a voice from higher up in the stands called the referee a 'dozy spanner' (you wouldn't hear that at the Emirates) – basically so many of the ingredients we had missed throughout the enforced absence. During the game we heard the first spontaneous loud cheer from the fans for a long time. Unfortunately, it came from the away end and signalled a goal for the opposition, a looping header from Burton's captain. Town picked up the tempo in the second half and did look more promising but the visitors' back four held firm with some stout defensive work.

Even though Shrewsbury had lost 1-0, in the great scheme of things, maybe the result didn't matter so much today, we were just so pleased to be back. Playing in the second tier again seems a long way off, on some distant horizon, and back in the late 70s many had similar thoughts, wondering if they would ever see their local club play at that level, but it happened, and Shrewsbury Town, after that wobbly start, went on to thrive in the Second Division. It can happen again. Floreat Salopia!

Afterword

Since the day in May 1980 when I pulled out the last voucher from my £12 junior season ticket and handed it over to the Meadow turnstile operator for the game against Fulham, I've been to countless matches that haven't involved a team in blue and amber from Shropshire. At different times, wherever I've fetched up, I've followed the fortunes and cheered on the likes of Leeds United, PAOK of Thessaloniki, Crystal Palace, Aston Villa and Leamington Brakes. I'm lucky enough to have attended a European Cup Final, an FA Cup Final, a Malaysian Cup Final, two World Cups and an overseas Euros. I've seen fire trucks deploying water cannons to repel rioters on the terraces of Śląsk Wrocław. I've watched Johan Cruyff execute a sublime pass down the line for his Dutch team-mate at Wembley and been offered Ferrero Rocher chocolates by a Yeovil fan in a tiny stand under the lights at Solihull Moors, whose team were about to suffer a cup upset. Yet nothing I've witnessed compares to the exhilarating pleasure of supporting my local team, Shrewsbury Town, during that magnificent period from the late 1970s to the dawn of the 80s.

Acknowledgements

A BIG thank you to Jake King and his wife Linda, for inviting me to their home and providing some first-hand insights on those wonderful times. And coffee. To Ian Whitfield for allowing me to make regular contributions about the 79/80 season in the Town programmes in 2019/20. To Jack Holland, the Texan Shrew, for his enthusiastic responses to those pieces. To Mike Jones and Kevin Davies for *Breathe on 'em Salop*, an invaluable resource. To the *Shropshire Star* for supplying Town updates and match reports over the years. Essential reading. To Matthew Ashton for offering some initial advice on the project. To Stuart Dunn, of BBC Radio Shropshire for his encouragement and for suggesting a meeting with Jake King. To Brian Caldwell, Shrewsbury Town Chief Executive and Company Secretary, for his backing. To Paul and all at Pitch Publishing for supporting the proposal and taking it to the next level.

To Steven for being there at the outset and at some of those glorious Gay Meadow occasions as well as coming along to more recent big games (when Leeds aren't playing). To my close, proud Salopian mates, Andrew Griffiths and Gerald Jones, for being willing Town compadres in the past and present (except when play-off finals fall in half-term week), and for sharing their memories. To Laura, to Eleanor and all the other relatives, friends and colleagues who have joined me for Town games. It's been emotional. And lastly, much love and thanks to Jo, who is always cool when I say I might be off to Shrewsbury, Wycombe, Accrington.

Bibliography

Dunn, S., 'Our Best Yet: Boss Quinn' *The Non-League Paper* (23 November 2003)

Housman, A.E., *A Shropshire Lad* (London: Harrap, 1984)

Jones, M., *Breathe on 'em Salop! Shrewsbury Town FC The Official History* (Harefield: Yore Publications, 1995)

Lansley, P., 'Shrewsbury strike late to make life grim and Grimmer for Wednesday' *Sunday Times* (31 January 2016)

Match

The Marshall Cavendish Football Handbook

Munro, J., 'Precious JEM' *Sunday Times* (5 January 2003)

Poole, A., 'Sorry New Year' *Coventry Telegraph* (2 January 2013)

Shoot!

Shropshire Star match reports and headlines (3 February 1975, 20 January 1978, 23 January 1978, 13 February 1978, 27 February 1978, 17 September 1979, 1 October 1979)

Whatever Happened to The Likely Lads? S1 E05: 'I'll Never Forget Whatshername', 6 February 1973

Winter, H., 'Zola tames the Shrews' *Daily Telegraph* (27 January 2003)

– Various Shrewsbury Town home and away club programmes and special editions, 1973–2021

Also available at all good book stores

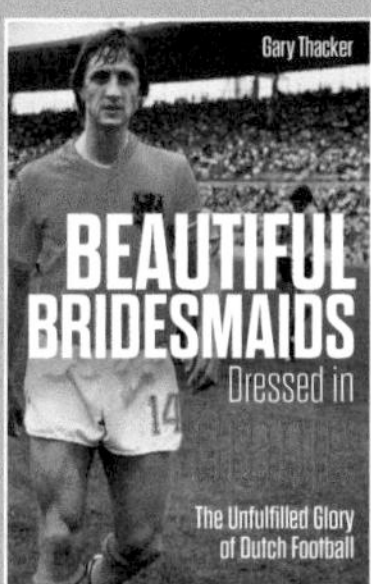

9781785318467

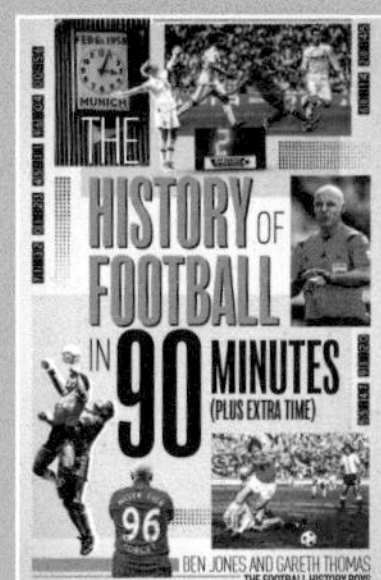

9781785318399

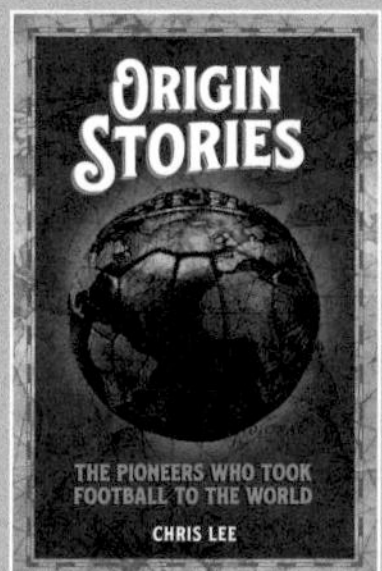

9781785317699

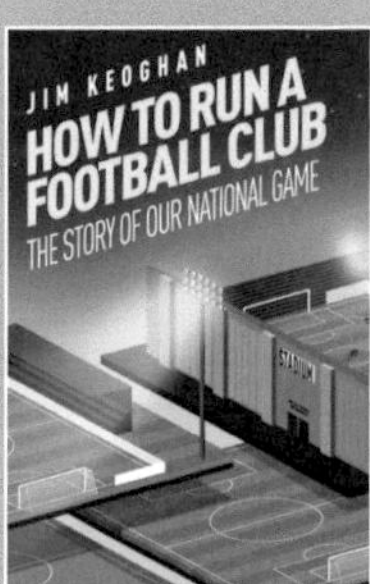

9781785316449

9781785316708

9781785316463

9781785316791

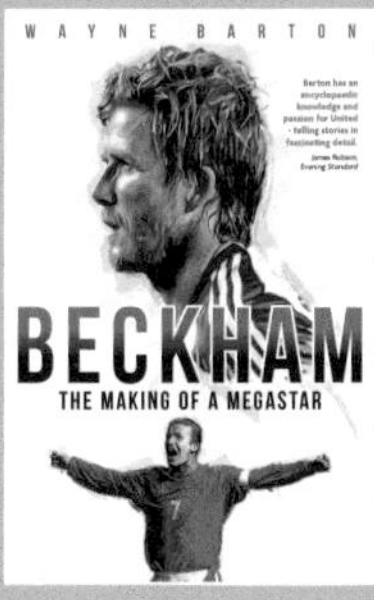

9781785316760

9781785316814